IVANOFF, A PLAY

ANTON CHEKHOV

CHARACTERS

NICHOLAS IVANOFF, perpetual member of the Council of Peasant Affairs

ANNA, his wife. Nee Sarah Abramson

MATTHEW SHABELSKI, a count, uncle of Ivanoff

PAUL LEBEDIEFF, President of the Board of the Zemstvo

ZINAIDA, his wife

SASHA, their daughter, twenty years old

LVOFF, a young government doctor

MARTHA BABAKINA, a young widow, owner of an estate and daughter of a rich merchant

KOSICH, an exciseman

MICHAEL BORKIN, a distant relative of Ivanoff, and manager of his estate

AVDOTIA NAZAROVNA, an old woman

GEORGE, lives with the Lebedieffs

FIRST GUEST SECOND GUEST THIRD GUEST FOURTH GUEST

PETER, a servant of Ivanoff

GABRIEL, a servant of Lebedieff

GUESTS OF BOTH SEXES

The play takes place in one of the provinces of central Russia

IVANOFF

ACT I

The garden of IVANOFF'S country place. On the left is a terrace and the facade of the house. One window is open. Below the terrace is a broad semicircular lawn, from which paths lead to right and left into a garden. On the right are several garden benches and tables. A lamp is burning on one of the tables. It is evening. As the curtain rises sounds of the piano and violoncello are heard.

IVANOFF is sitting at a table reading.

BORKIN, in top-boots and carrying a gun, comes in from the rear of the garden. He is a little tipsy. As he sees IVANOFF he comes toward him on tiptoe, and when he comes opposite him he stops and points the gun at his face.

IVANOFF. [Catches sight of BORKIN. Shudders and jumps to his feet] Misha! What are you doing? You frightened me! I can't stand your stupid jokes when I am so nervous as this. And having frightened me, you laugh! [He sits down.]

BORKIN. [Laughing loudly] There, I am sorry, really. I won't do it again. Indeed I won't. [Take off his cap] How hot it is! Just think, my dear boy, I have covered twelve miles in the last three hours. I am worn out. Just feel how my heart is beating.

IVANOFF. [Goes on reading] Oh, very well. I shall feel it later!

BORKIN. No, feel it now. [He takes IVANOFF'S hand and presses it against his breast] Can you feel it thumping? That means that it is weak and that I may die suddenly at any moment. Would you be sorry if I died?

IVANOFF. I am reading now. I shall attend to you later.

BORKIN. No, seriously, would you be sorry if I died? Nicholas, would you be sorry if I died?

IVANOFF. Leave me alone!

BORKIN. Come, tell me if you would be sorry or not.

IVANOFF. I am sorry that you smell so of vodka, Misha, it is disgusting.

BORKIN. Do I smell of vodka? How strange! And yet, it is not so strange after all. I met the magistrate on the road, and I must admit that we did drink about eight glasses together. Strictly speaking, of course, drinking is very harmful. Listen, it is harmful, isn't it? Is it? Is it?

IVANOFF. This is unendurable! Let me warn you, Misha, that you are going too far.

BORKIN. Well, well, excuse me. Sit here by yourself then, for heaven's sake, if it amuses you. [Gets up and goes away] What extraordinary people one meets in the world. They won't even allow themselves to be spoken to. [He comes back] Oh, yes, I nearly forgot. Please let me have eighty-two roubles.

IVANOFF. Why do you want eighty-two roubles?

BORKIN. To pay the workmen to-morrow.

IVANOFF. I haven't the money.

BORKIN. Many thanks. [Angrily] So you haven't the money! And yet the workmen must be paid, mustn't they?

IVANOFF. I don't know. Wait till my salary comes in on the first of the month.

BORKIN. How is it possible to discuss anything with a man like you? Can't you understand that the workmen are coming to-morrow morning and not on the first of the month?

IVANOFF. How can I help it? I'll be hanged if I can do anything about it now. And what do you mean by this irritating way you have of pestering me whenever I am trying to read or write or——

BORKIN. Must the workmen be paid or not, I ask you? But, good gracious! What is the use of talking to you! [Waves his hand] Do you think because you own an estate you can command the whole world? With your two thousand acres and your empty pockets you are like a man who has a cellar full of wine and no corkscrew. I have sold the oats as they stand in the field. Yes, sir! And to-morrow I shall sell the rye and the carriage horses. [He stamps up and down] Do you think I am going to stand upon ceremony with you? Certainly not! I am not that kind of a man!

ANNA appears at the open window.

ANNA. Whose voice did I hear just now? Was it yours, Misha? Why are you stamping up and down?

BORKIN. Anybody who had anything to do with your Nicholas would stamp up and down.

ANNA. Listen, Misha! Please have some hay carried onto the croquet lawn.

BORKIN. [Waves his hand] Leave me alone, please!

ANNA. Oh, what manners! They are not becoming to you at all. If you want to be liked by women you must never let them see you when you are angry or obstinate. [To her husband] Nicholas, let us go and play on the lawn in the hay!

IVANOFF. Don't you know it is bad for you to stand at the open window, Annie? [Calls] Shut the window, Uncle!

[The window is shut from the inside.]

BORKIN. Don't forget that the interest on the money you owe Lebedieff must be paid in two days.

IVANOFF. I haven't forgotten it. I am going over to see Lebedieff today and shall ask him to wait.

[He looks at his watch.]

BORKIN. When are you going?

IVANOFF. At once.

BORKIN. Wait! Wait! Isn't this Sasha's birthday? So it is! The idea of my forgetting it. What a memory I have. [Jumps about] I shall go with you! [Sings] I shall go, I shall go! Nicholas, old man, you are the joy of my life. If you were not always so nervous and cross and gloomy, you and I could do great things together. I would do anything for you. Shall I marry Martha Babakina and give you half her fortune? That is, not half, either, but all—take it all!

IVANOFF. Enough of this nonsense!

BORKIN. No, seriously, shan't I marry Martha and halve the money with you? But no, why should I propose it? How can you understand? [Angrily] You say to me: "Stop talking nonsense!" You are a good man and a clever one, but you haven't any red blood in your veins or any—well, enthusiasm. Why, if you wanted to, you and I could cut a dash together that would shame the devil himself. If you were a normal man instead of a morbid hypochondriac we would have a million in a year. For instance, if I had twenty-three hundred roubles now I could make twenty thousand in two weeks. You don't believe me? You think it is all nonsense? No, it isn't nonsense. Give me twenty-three hundred roubles and let me try. Ofsianoff is selling a strip of land across the river for that price. If we buy this, both banks will be ours, and we shall have the right to build a dam across the river. Isn't that so? We can say that we intend to build a mill, and when the people on the river below us hear that we mean to dam the river they will, of course, object violently and we shall say: If you don't want a dam here you will have to pay to get us away. Do you see the result? The factory would give us five thousand roubles, Korolkoff three thousand, the monastery five thousand more—

IVANOFF. All that is simply idiotic, Misha. If you don't want me to lose my temper you must keep your schemes to yourself.

BORKIN. [Sits down at the table] Of course! I knew how it would be! You never will act for yourself, and you tie my hands so that I am helpless.

Enter SHABELSKI and LVOFF.

SHABELSKI. The only difference between lawyers and doctors is that lawyers simply rob you, whereas doctors both rob you and kill you. I am not referring to any one present. [Sits down on the bench] They are all frauds and swindlers. Perhaps in Arcadia you might find an exception to the general rule and yet—I have treated thousands of sick people myself in my life, and I have never met a doctor who did not seem to me to be an unmistakable scoundrel.

BORKIN. [To IVANOFF] Yes, you tie my hands and never do anything for yourself, and that is why you have no money.

SHABELSKI. As I said before, I am not referring to any one here at present; there may be exceptions though, after all—[He yawns.]

IVANOFF. [Shuts his book] What have you to tell me, doctor?

LVOFF. [Looks toward the window] Exactly what I said this morning: she must go to the Crimea at once. [Walks up and down.]

SHABELSKI. [Bursts out laughing] To the Crimea! Why don't you and I set up as doctors, Misha? Then, if some Madame Angot or Ophelia finds the world tiresome and begins to cough and be consumptive, all we shall have to do will be to write out a prescription according to the laws of medicine: that is, first, we shall order her a young doctor, and then a journey to the Crimea. There some fascinating young Tartar——

IVANOFF. [Interrupting] Oh, don't be coarse! [To LVOFF] It takes money to go to the Crimea, and even if I could afford it, you know she has refused to go.

LVOFF. Yes, she has. [A pause.]

BORKIN. Look here, doctor, is Anna really so ill that she absolutely must go to the Crimea?

LVOFF. [Looking toward the window] Yes, she has consumption.

BORKIN. Whew! How sad! I have seen in her face for some time that she could not last much longer.

LVOFF. Can't you speak quietly? She can hear everything you say. [A pause.]

BORKIN. [Sighing] The life of man is like a flower, blooming so gaily in a field. Then, along comes a goat, he eats it, and the flower is gone!

SHABELSKI. Oh, nonsense, nonsense. [Yawning] Everything is a fraud and a swindle. [A pause.]

BORKIN. Gentlemen, I have been trying to tell Nicholas how he can make some money, and have submitted a brilliant plan to him, but my seed, as usual, has fallen on barren soil. Look what a sight he is now: dull, cross, bored, peevish——

SHABELSKI. [Gets up and stretches himself] You are always inventing schemes for everybody, you clever fellow, and telling them how to live; can't you tell me something? Give me some good advice, you ingenious young man. Show me a good move to make.

BORKIN. [Getting up] I am going to have a swim. Goodbye, gentlemen. [To Shabelski] There are at least twenty good moves you could make. If I were you I should have twenty thousand roubles in a week.

[He goes out; SHABELSKI follows him.]

SHABELSKI. How would you do it? Come, explain.

BORKIN. There is nothing to explain, it is so simple. [Coming back] Nicholas, give me a rouble.

IVANOFF silently hands him the money

BORKIN. Thanks. Shabelski, you still hold some trump cards.

SHABELSKI follows him out.

SHABELSKI. Well, what are they?

BORKIN. If I were you I should have thirty thousand roubles and more in a week. [They go out together.]

IVANOFF. [After a pause] Useless people, useless talk, and the necessity of answering stupid questions, have wearied me so, doctor, that I am ill. I have become so irritable and bitter that I don't know myself. My head aches for days at a time. I hear a ringing in my ears, I can't sleep, and yet there is no escape from it all, absolutely none.

LVOFF. Ivanoff, I have something serious to speak to you about.

IVANOFF. What is it?

LVOFF. It is about your wife. She refuses to go to the Crimea alone, but she would go with you.

IVANOFF. [Thoughtfully] It would cost a great deal for us both to go, and besides, I could not get leave to be away for so long. I have had one holiday already this year.

LVOFF. Very well, let us admit that. Now to proceed. The best cure for consumption is absolute peace of mind, and your wife has none whatever. She is forever excited by your behaviour to her. Forgive me, I am excited and am going to speak frankly. Your treatment of her is killing her. [A pause] Ivanoff, let me believe better things of you.

IVANOFF. What you say is true, true. I must be terribly guilty, but my mind is confused. My will seems to be paralysed by a kind of stupor; I can't understand myself or any one else. [Looks toward the window] Come, let us take a walk, we might be overheard here. [They get up] My dear friend, you should hear the whole story from the beginning if it were not so long and complicated that to tell it would take all night. [They walk up and down] Anna is a splendid, an exceptional woman. She has left her faith, her parents and her fortune for my sake. If I should demand a hundred other sacrifices, she would consent to every one without the quiver of an eyelid. Well, I am not a remarkable man in any way, and have sacrificed nothing. However, the story is a long one. In short, the whole point is, my dear doctor—[Confused] that I married her for love and promised to love her forever, and now after five years she loves me still and I—[He waves his hand] Now, when you tell me she is dying, I feel neither love nor pity, only a sort of loneliness and weariness. To all appearances this must seem horrible, and I cannot understand myself what is happening to me. [They go out.]

SHABELSKI comes in.

SHABELSKI. [Laughing] Upon my word, that man is no scoundrel, but a great thinker, a master-mind. He deserves a memorial. He is the essence of modern ingenuity, and combines in himself alone the genius of the lawyer, the doctor, and the financier. [He sits down on the lowest step of the terrace] And yet he has never finished a course of studies in any college; that is so surprising. What an ideal scoundrel he would have made if he had acquired a little culture and mastered the sciences! "You could make twenty thousand roubles in a week," he said. "You still hold the ace of trumps: it is your title." [Laughing] He said I might get a rich girl to marry me for it! [ANNA opens the window and looks down] "Let me make a match between you and Martha," says he. Who is this Martha? It must be that Balabalkina—Babakalkina woman, the one that looks like a laundress.

ANNA. Is that you, Count?

SHABELSKI. What do you want?

ANNA laughs.

SHABELSKI. [With a Jewish accent] Vy do you laugh?

ANNA. I was thinking of something you said at dinner, do you remember? How was it—a forgiven thief, a doctored horse.

SHABELSKI. A forgiven thief, a doctored horse, and a Christianised Jew are all worth the same price.

ANNA. [Laughing] You can't even repeat the simplest saying without ill-nature. You are a most malicious old man. [Seriously] Seriously, Count you are extremely disagreeable, and very tiresome and painful to live with. You are always grumbling and growling, and everybody to you is a blackguard and a scoundrel. Tell me honestly, Count, have you ever spoken well of any one?

SHABELSKI. Is this an inquisition?

ANNA. We have lived under this same roof now for five years, and I have never heard you speak kindly of people, or without bitterness and derision. What harm has the world done to you? Is it possible that you consider yourself better than any one else?

SHABELSKI. Not at all. I think we are all of us scoundrels and hypocrites. I myself am a degraded old man, and as useless as a cast-off shoe. I abuse myself as much as any one else. I was rich once, and free, and happy at times, but now I am a dependent, an object of charity, a joke to the world. When I am at last exasperated and defy them, they answer me with a laugh. When I laugh, they shake their heads sadly and say, "The old man has gone mad." But oftenest of all I am unheard and unnoticed by every one.

ANNA. [Quietly] Screaming again.

SHABELSKI. Who is screaming?

ANNA. The owl. It screams every evening.

SHABELSKI. Let it scream. Things are as bad as they can be already. [Stretches himself] Alas, my dear Sarah! If I could only win a thousand or two roubles, I should soon show you what I could do. I wish you could see me! I should get away out of this hole, and leave the bread of charity, and should not show my nose here again until the last judgment day.

ANNA. What would you do if you were to win so much money?

SHABELSKI. [Thoughtfully] First I would go to Moscow to hear the Gipsies play, and then—then I should fly to Paris and take an apartment and go to the Russian Church.

ANNA. And what else?

SHABELSKI. I would go and sit on my wife's grave for days and days and think. I would sit there until I died. My wife is buried in Paris. [A pause.]

ANNA. How terribly dull this is! Shall we play a duet?

SHABELSKI. As you like. Go and get the music ready. [ANNA goes out.]

IVANOFF and LVOFF appear in one of the paths.

IVANOFF. My dear friend, you left college last year, and you are still young and brave. Being thirty-five years old I have the right to advise you. Don't marry a Jewess or a bluestocking or a woman who is queer in any way. Choose some nice, common-place girl without any strange and startling points in her character. Plan your life for quiet; the greyer and more monotonous you can make the background, the better. My dear boy, do not try to fight alone against thousands; do not tilt with windmills; do not dash yourself against the rocks. And, above all, may you be spared the so-called rational life, all wild theories and impassioned talk. Everything is in the hands of God, so shut yourself up in your shell and do your best. That is the pleasant, honest, healthy way to live. But the life I have chosen has been so tiring, oh, so tiring! So full of mistakes, of injustice and stupidity! [Catches sight of SHABELSKI, and speaks angrily] There you are again, Uncle, always under foot, never letting one have a moment's quiet talk!

SHABELSKI. [In a tearful voice] Is there no refuge anywhere for a poor old devil like me? [He jumps up and runs into the house.]

IVANOFF. Now I have offended him! Yes, my nerves have certainly gone to pieces. I must do something about it, I must——

LVOFF. [Excitedly] Ivanoff, I have heard all you have to say and—and—I am going to speak frankly. You have shown me in your voice and manner, as well as in your words, the most heartless egotism and pitiless cruelty. Your nearest friend is dying simply because she is near you, her days are numbered, and you can feel such indifference that you go about giving advice and analysing your feelings. I cannot say all I should like to; I have not the gift of words, but—but I can at least say that you are deeply antipathetic to me.

IVANOFF. I suppose I am. As an onlooker, of course you see me more clearly than I see myself, and your judgment of me is probably right. No doubt I am terribly guilty. [Listens] I think I hear the carriage coming. I must get ready to go. [He goes toward the house and then stops] You dislike me, doctor, and you don't conceal it. Your sincerity does you credit. [He goes into the house.]

LVOFF. [Alone] What a confoundedly disagreeable character! I have let another opportunity slip without speaking to him as I meant to, but I simply cannot talk calmly to that man. The moment I open my mouth to speak I feel such a commotion and suffocation here [He puts his hand on his breast] that my tongue sticks to the roof of my mouth. Oh, I loathe that Tartuffe, that unmitigated rascal, with all my heart! There he is, preparing to go driving in spite of the entreaties of his unfortunate wife, who adores him and whose only happiness is his presence. She implores him to spend at least one evening with her, and he cannot even do that. Why, he might shoot himself in despair if he had to stay at home! Poor fellow, what he wants are new fields for his villainous schemes. Oh, I know why you go to Lebedieff's every evening, Ivanoff! I know.

Enter IVANOFF, in hat and coat, ANNA and SHABELSKI

SHABELSKI. Look here, Nicholas, this is simply barbarous You go away every evening and leave us here alone, and we get so bored that we have to go to bed at eight o'clock. It is a scandal, and no decent way of living. Why can you go driving if we can't? Why?

ANNA. Leave him alone, Count. Let him go if he wants to.

IVANOFF. How can a sick woman like you go anywhere? You know you have a cough and must not go out after sunset. Ask the doctor here. You are no child, Annie, you must be reasonable. And as for you, what would you do with yourself over there?

SHABELSKI. I am ready to go anywhere: into the jaws of a crocodile, or even into the jaws of hell, so long as I don't have to stay here. I am horribly bored. I am stupefied by this dullness. Every one here is tired of me. You leave me at home to entertain Anna, but I feel more like scratching and biting her.

ANNA. Leave him alone, Count. Leave him alone. Let him go if he enjoys himself there.

IVANOFF. What does this mean, Annie? You know I am not going for pleasure. I must see Lebedieff about the money I owe him.

ANNA. I don't see why you need justify yourself to me. Go ahead! Who is keeping you?

IVANOFF. Heavens! Don't let us bite one another's heads off. Is that really unavoidable?

SHABELSKI. [Tearfully] Nicholas, my dear boy, do please take me with you. I might possibly be amused a little by the sight of all the fools and scoundrels I should see there. You know I haven't been off this place since Easter.

IVANOFF. [Exasperated] Oh, very well! Come along then! How tiresome you all are!

SHABELSKI. I may go? Oh, thank you! [Takes him gaily by the arm and leads him aside] May I wear your straw hat?

IVANOFF. You may, only hurry, please.

SHABELSKI runs into the house.

IVANOFF. How tired I am of you all! But no, what am I saying? Annie, my manner to you is insufferable, and it never used to be. Well, good-bye, Annie. I shall be back by one.

ANNA. Nicholas! My dear husband, stay at home to-night!

IVANOFF. [Excitedly] Darling, sweetheart, my dear, unhappy one, I implore you to let me leave home in the evenings. I know it is cruel and unjust to ask this, but let me do you this injustice. It is such torture for me to stay. As soon as the sun goes down my soul is overwhelmed by the most horrible despair. Don't ask me why; I don't know; I swear I don't. This dreadful melancholy torments me here, it drives me to the Lebedieff's and there it grows worse than ever. I rush home; it still pursues me; and so I am tortured all through the night. It is breaking my heart.

ANNA. Nicholas, won't you stay? We will talk together as we used to. We will have supper together and read afterward. The old grumbler and I have learned so many duets to play to you. [She kisses him. Then, after a pause] I can't understand you any more. This has been going on for a year now. What has changed you so?

IVANOFF. I don't know.

ANNA. And why don't you want me to go driving with you in the evening?

IVANOFF. As you insist on knowing, I shall have to tell you. It is a little cruel, but you had best understand. When this melancholy fit is on me I begin to dislike you, Annie, and at such times I must escape from you. In short, I simply have to leave this house.

ANNA. Oh, you are sad, are you? I can understand that! Nicholas, let me tell you something: won't you try to sing and laugh and scold as you used to? Stay here, and we will drink some liqueur together, and laugh, and chase away this sadness of yours in no time. Shall I sing to you? Or shall we sit in your study in the twilight as we used to, while you tell me about your sadness? I can read such suffering in your eyes! Let me look into them and weep, and our hearts will both be lighter. [She laughs and cries at once] Or is it really true that the flowers return with every spring, but lost happiness never returns? Oh, is it? Well, go then, go!

IVANOFF. Pray for me, Annie! [He goes; then stops and thinks for a moment] No, I can't do it. [IVANOFF goes out.]

ANNA. Yes, go, go—[Sits down at the table.]

LVOFF. [Walking up and down] Make this a rule, Madam: as soon as the sun goes down you must go indoors and not come out again until morning. The damp evening air is bad for you.

ANNA. Yes, sir!

LVOFF. What do you mean by "Yes, sir"? I am speaking seriously.

ANNA. But I don't want to be serious. [She coughs.]

LVOFF. There now, you see, you are coughing already.

SHABELSKI comes out of the house in his hat and coat.

SHABELSKI. Where is Nicholas? Is the carriage here yet? [Goes quickly to ANNA and kisses her hand] Good-night, my darling! [Makes a face and speaks with a Jewish accent] I beg your bardon! [He goes quickly out.]

LVOFF. Idiot!

A pause; the sounds of a concertina are heard in the distance.

ANNA. Oh, how lonely it is! The coachman and the cook are having a little ball in there by themselves, and I—I am, as it were, abandoned. Why are you walking about, Doctor? Come and sit down here.

LVOFF. I can't sit down.

[A pause.]

ANNA. They are playing "The Sparrow" in the kitchen. [She sings]

```
"Sparrow, Sparrow, where are you?
 On the mountain drinking dew."
```

[A pause] Are your father and mother living, Doctor?

LVOFF. My mother is living; my father is dead.

ANNA. Do you miss your mother very much?

LVOFF. I am too busy to miss any one.

ANNA. [Laughing] The flowers return with every spring, but lost happiness never returns. I wonder who taught me that? I think it was Nicholas himself. [Listens] The owl is hooting again.

LVOFF. Well, let it hoot.

ANNA. I have begun to think, Doctor, that fate has cheated me. Other people who, perhaps, are no better than I am are happy and have not had to pay for their happiness. But I have paid for it all, every moment of it, and such a price! Why should I have to pay so terribly? Dear friend, you are all too considerate and gentle with me to tell me the truth; but do you think I don't know what is the matter with me? I know perfectly well. However, this isn't a pleasant subject—[With a Jewish accent] "I beg your bardon!" Can you tell funny stories?

LVOFF. No, I can't.

ANNA. Nicholas can. I am beginning to be surprised, too, at the injustice of people. Why do they return hatred for love, and answer truth with lies? Can you tell me how much longer I shall be hated by my mother and father? They live fifty miles away, and yet I can feel their hatred day and night, even in my sleep. And how do you account for the sadness of Nicholas? He says that he only dislikes me in the evening, when the fit is on him. I understand that, and can tolerate it, but what if he should come to dislike me altogether? Of course that is impossible, and yet—no, no, I mustn't even imagine such a thing. [Sings]

```
"Sparrow, Sparrow, where are you?"
```

[She shudders] What fearful thoughts I have! You are not married, Doctor; there are many things that you cannot understand.

LVOFF. You say you are surprised, but—but it is you who surprise me. Tell me, explain to me how you, an honest and intelligent woman, almost a saint, could allow yourself to be so basely deceived and dragged into this den of bears? Why are you here? What have you in common with such a cold and heartless—but enough of your husband! What have you in common with these wicked and vulgar surroundings? With that eternal grumbler, the crazy and decrepit Count? With that swindler, that prince of rascals, Misha, with his fool's face? Tell me, I say, how did you get here?

ANNA. [laughing] That is what he used to say, long ago, oh, exactly! Only his eyes are larger than yours, and when he was excited they used to shine like coals—go on, go on!

LVOFF. [Gets up and waves his hand] There is nothing more to say. Go into the house.

ANNA. You say that Nicholas is not what he should be, that his faults are so and so. How can you possibly understand him? How can you learn to know any one in six months? He is a wonderful man, Doctor, and I am sorry you could not have known him as he was two or three years ago. He is depressed and silent now, and broods all day without doing anything, but he was splendid then. I fell in love with him at first sight. [Laughing] I gave one look and was caught like a mouse in a trap! So when he asked me to go with him I cut every tie that bound me to my old life as one snips the withered leaves from a plant. But things are different now. Now he goes to the Lebedieff's to amuse himself with other women, and I sit here in the garden and listen to the owls. [The WATCHMAN'S rattle is heard] Tell me, Doctor, have you any brothers and sisters?

LVOFF. No.

ANNA sobs.

LVOFF. What is it? What is the matter?

ANNA. I can't stand it, Doctor, I must go.

LVOFF. Where?

ANNA. To him. I am going. Have the horses harnessed. [She runs into the house.]

LVOFF. No, I certainly cannot go on treating any one under these conditions. I not only have to do it for nothing, but I am forced to endure this agony of mind besides. No, no, I can't stand it. I have had enough of it. [He goes into the house.]

The curtain falls.

ACT II

The drawing-room of LEBEDIEFFŌS house. In the centre is a door leading into a garden. Doors open out of the room to the right and left. The room is furnished with valuable old furniture, which is carefully protected by linen covers. The walls are hung with pictures. The room is lighted by candelabra. ZINAIDA is sitting on a sofa; the elderly guests are sitting in arm-chairs on either hand. The young guests are sitting about the room on small chairs. KOSICH, AVDOTIA NAZAROVNA, GEORGE, and others are playing cards in the background. GABRIEL is standing near the door on the right. The maid is passing sweetmeats about on a tray. During the entire act guests come and go from the garden, through the room, out of the door on the left, and back again. Enter MARTHA through the door on the right. She goes toward ZINAIDA.

ZINAIDA. [Gaily] My dearest Martha!

MARTHA. How do you do, Zinaida? Let me congratulate you on your daughter's birthday.

ZINAIDA. Thank you, my dear; I am delighted to see you. How are you?

MARTHA. Very well indeed, thank you. [She sits down on the sofa] Good evening, young people!

The younger guests get up and bow.

FIRST GUEST. [Laughing] Young people indeed! Do you call yourself an old person?

MARTHA. [Sighing] How can I make any pretense to youth now?

FIRST GUEST. What nonsense! The fact that you are a widow means nothing. You could beat any pretty girl you chose at a canter.

GABRIEL brings MARTHA some tea.

ZINAIDA. Why do you bring the tea in like that? Go and fetch some jam to eat with it!

MARTHA. No thank you; none for me, don't trouble yourself. [A pause.]

FIRST GUEST. [To MARTHA] Did you come through Mushkine on your way here?

MARTHA. No, I came by way of Spassk. The road is better that way.

FIRST GUEST. Yes, so it is.

KOSICH. Two in spades.

GEORGE. Pass.

AVDOTIA. Pass.

SECOND GUEST. Pass.

MARTHA. The price of lottery tickets has gone up again, my dear. I have never known such a state of affairs. The first issue is already worth two hundred and seventy and the second nearly two hundred and fifty. This has never happened before.

ZINAIDA. How fortunate for those who have a great many tickets!

MARTHA. Don't say that, dear; even when the price of tickets is high it does not pay to put one's capital into them.

ZINAIDA. Quite true, and yet, my dear, one never can tell what may happen. Providence is sometimes kind.

THIRD GUEST. My impression is, ladies, that at present capital is exceedingly unproductive. Shares pay very small dividends, and speculating is exceedingly dangerous. As I understand it, the capitalist now finds himself in a more critical position than the man who——

MARTHA. Quite right.

FIRST GUEST yawns.

MARTHA. How dare you yawn in the presence of ladies?

FIRST GUEST. I beg your pardon! It was quite an accident.

ZINAIDA gets up and goes out through the door on the right.

GEORGE. Two in hearts.

SECOND GUEST. Pass.

KOSICH. Pass.

MARTHA. [Aside] Heavens! This is deadly! I shall die of ennui.

Enter ZINAIDA and LEBEDIEFF through the door on the right.

ZINAIDA. Why do you go off by yourself like a prima donna? Come and sit with our guests!

[She sits down in her former place.]

LEBEDIEFF. [Yawning] Oh, dear, our sins are heavy! [He catches sight of MARTHA] Why, there is my little sugar-plum! How is your most esteemed highness?

MARTHA. Very well, thank you.

LEBEDIEFF. Splendid, splendid! [He sits down in an armchair] Quite right—Oh, Gabriel!

GABRIEL brings him a glass of vodka and a tumbler of water. He empties the glass of vodka and sips the water.

FIRST GUEST. Good health to you!

LEBEDIEFF. Good health is too much to ask. I am content to keep death from the door. [To his wife] Where is the heroine of this occasion, Zuzu?

KOSICH. [In a plaintive voice] Look here, why haven't we taken any tricks yet? [He jumps up] Yes, why have we lost this game entirely, confound it?

AVDOTIA. [Jumps up angrily] Because, friend, you don't know how to play it, and have no right to be sitting here at all. What right had you to lead from another suit? Haven't you the ace left? [They both leave the table and run forward.]

KOSICH. [In a tearful voice] Ladies and gentlemen, let me explain! I had the ace, king, queen, and eight of diamonds, the ace of spades and one, just one, little heart, do you understand? Well, she, bad luck to her, she couldn't make a little slam. I said one in no-trumps—— *

> * The game played is vint, the national card-game of Russia and the direct ancestor of auction bridge, with which it is almost identical.

AVDOTIA. [Interrupting him] No, I said one in no-trumps; you said two in no-trumps——

KOSICH. This is unbearable! Allow me—you had—I had—you had—[To LEBEDIEFF] But you shall decide it, Paul: I had the ace, king, queen, and eight of diamonds——

LEBEDIEFF. [Puts his fingers into his ears] Stop, for heaven's sake, stop!

AVDOTIA. [Yelling] I said no-trumps, and not he!

KOSICH. [Furiously] I'll be damned if I ever sit down to another game of cards with that old cat!

He rushes into the garden. The SECOND GUEST follows him. GEORGE is left alone at the table.

AVDOTIA. Whew! He makes my blood boil! Old cat, indeed! You're an old cat yourself!

MARTHA. How angry you are, aunty!

AVDOTIA. [Sees MARTHA and claps her hands] Are you here, my darling? My beauty! And was I blind as a bat, and didn't see you? Darling child! [She kisses her and sits down beside her] How happy this makes me! Let me feast my eyes on you, my milk-white swan! Oh, oh, you have bewitched me!

LEBEDIEFF. Why don't you find her a husband instead of singing her praises?

AVDOTIA. He shall be found. I shall not go to my grave before I have found a husband for her, and one for Sasha too. I shall not go to my grave—[She sighs] But where to find these husbands nowadays? There sit some possible bridegrooms now, huddled together like a lot of half-drowned rats!

THIRD GUEST. A most unfortunate comparison! It is my belief, ladies, that if the young men of our day prefer to remain single, the fault lies not with them, but with the existing, social conditions!

LEBEDIEFF. Come, enough of that! Don't give us any mo re philosophy; I don't like it!

Enter SASHA. She goes up to her father.

SASHA. How can you endure the stuffy air of this room when the weather is so beautiful?

ZINAIDA. My dear Sasha, don't you see that Martha is here?

SASHA. I beg your pardon.

[She goes up to MARTHA and shakes hands.]

MARTHA. Yes, here I am, my dear little Sasha, and proud to congratulate you. [They kiss each other] Many happy returns of the day, dear!

SASHA. Thank you! [She goes and sits down by her father.]

LEBEDIEFF. As you were saying, Avdotia Nazarovna, husbands are hard to find. I don't want to be rude, but I must say that the young men of the present are a dull and poky lot, poor fellows! They can't dance or talk or drink as they should do.

AVDOTIA. Oh, as far as drinking goes, they are all experts. Just give them—give them——

LEBEDIEFF. Simply to drink is no art. A horse can drink. No, it must be done in the right way. In my young days we used to sit and cudgel our brains all day over our lessons, but as soon as evening came we would fly off on some spree and keep it up till dawn. How we used to dance and flirt, and drink, too! Or sometimes we would sit and chatter and discuss everything under the sun until we almost wagged our tongues off. But now—[He waves his hand] Boys are a puzzle to me. They are not willing either to give a candle to God or a pitchfork to the devil! There is only one young fellow in the country who is worth a penny, and he is married. [Sighs] They say, too, that he is going crazy.

MARTHA. Who is he?

LEBEDIEFF. Nicholas Ivanoff.

MARTHA. Yes, he is a fine fellow, only [Makes a face] he is very unhappy.

ZINAIDA. How could he be otherwise, poor boy! [She sighs] He made such a bad mistake. When he married that Jewess of his he thought of course that her parents would give away whole mountains of gold with her, but, on the contrary, on the day she became a Christian they disowned her, and Ivanoff has never seen a penny of the money. He has repented of his folly now, but it is too late.

SASHA. Mother, that is not true!

MARTHA. How can you say it is not true, Sasha, when we all know it to be a fact? Why did he have to marry a Jewess? He must have had some reason for doing it. Are Russian girls so scarce? No, he made a mistake, poor fellow, a sad mistake. [Excitedly] And what on earth can he do with her now? Where could she go if he were to come home some day and say: "Your parents have deceived me; leave my house at once!" Her parents wouldn't take her back. She might find a place as a house-maid if she had ever learned to work, which she hasn't. He worries and worries her now, but the Count interferes. If it had not been for the Count, he would have worried her to death long ago.

AVDOTIA. They say he shuts her up in a cellar and stuffs her with garlic, and she eats and eats until her very soul reeks of it. [Laughter.]

SASHA. But, father, you know that isn't true!

LEBEDIEFF. What if it isn't, Sasha? Let them spin yarns if it amuses them. [He calls] Gabriel!

GABRIEL brings him another glass of vodka and a glass of water.

ZINAIDA. His misfortunes have almost ruined him, poor man. His affairs are in a frightful condition. If Borkin did not take such good charge of his estate he and his Jewess would soon be starving to death. [She sighs] And what anxiety he has caused us! Heaven only knows how we have suffered. Do you realise, my dear, that for three years he has owed us nine thousand roubles?

MARTHA. [Horrified] Nine thousand!

ZINAIDA. Yes, that is the sum that my dear Paul has undertaken to lend him. He never knows to whom it is safe to lend money and to whom it is not. I don't worry about the principal, but he ought to pay the interest on his debt.

SASHA. [Hotly] Mamma, you have already discussed this subject at least a thousand times!

ZINAIDA. What difference does it make to you? Why should you interfere?

SASHA. What is this mania you all have for gossiping about a man who has never done any of you any harm? Tell me, what harm has he done you?

THIRD GUEST. Let me say two words, Miss Sasha. I esteem Ivanoff, and have always found him an honourable man, but, between ourselves, I also consider him an adventurer.

SASHA. I congratulate you on your opinion!

THIRD GUEST. In proof of its truth, permit me to present to you the following facts, as they were communicated to me by his secretary, or shall I say rather, by his factotum, Borkin. Two years ago, at the time of the cattle plague, he bought some cattle and had them insured—

ZINAIDA. Yes, I remember hearing' of that.

THIRD GUEST. He had them insured, as you understand, and then inoculated them with the disease and claimed the insurance.

SASHA. Oh, what nonsense, nonsense, nonsense! No one bought or inoculated any cattle! The story was invented by Borkin, who then went about boasting of his clever plan. Ivanoff would not forgive Borkin for two weeks after he heard of it. He is only guilty of a weak character and too great faith in humanity. He can't make up his mind to get rid of that Borkin, and so all his possessions have been tricked and stolen from him. Every one who has had anything to do with Ivanoff has taken advantage of his generosity to grow rich.

LEBEDIEFF. Sasha, you little firebrand, that will do!

SASHA. Why do you all talk like this? This eternal subject of Ivanoff, Ivanoff, and always Ivanoff has grown insufferable, and yet you never speak of anything else. [She goes toward the door, then stops and comes back] I am surprised, [To the young men] and utterly astonished at your patience, young men! How can you sit there like that? Aren't you bored? Why, the very air is as dull as ditchwater! Do, for heaven's sake say something; try to amuse the girls a little, move about! Or if you can't talk of anything except Ivanoff, you might laugh or sing or dance——

LEBEDIEFF. [Laughing] That's right, Sasha! Give them a good scolding.

SASHA. Look here, will you do me a favour? If you refuse to dance or sing or laugh, if all that is tedious, then let me beg you, implore you, to summon all your powers, if only for this once, and make one witty or clever remark. Let it be as impertinent and malicious as you like, so long as it is funny and original. Won't you perform this miracle, just once, to surprise us and make us laugh? Or else you might think of some little thing which you could all do together, something to make you stir about. Let the girls admire you for once in their lives! Listen to me! I suppose you want them to like you? Then why don't try to make them do it? Oh, dear! There is something wrong with you all! You are a lot of sleepy stick-in-the-muds! I have told you so a thousand times and shall always go on repeating it; there is something wrong with every one of you; something wrong, wrong, wrong!

Enter IVANOFF and SHABELSKI through the door on the right.

SHABELSKI. Who is making a speech here? Is it you, Sasha? [He laughs and shakes hands with her] Many happy returns of the day, my dear child. May you live as long as possible in this life, but never be born again!

ZINAIDA. [Joyfully] My dear Count!

LEBEDIEFF. Who can this be? Not you, Count?

SHABELSKI. [Sees ZINAIDA and MARTHA sitting side by side] Two gold mines side by side! What a pleasant picture it makes! [He shakes hands with ZINAIDA] Good evening, Zuzu! [Shakes hands with MARTHA] Good evening, Birdie!

ZINAIDA. I am charmed to see you, Count. You are a rare visitor here now. [Calls] Gabriel, bring some tea! Please sit down.

She gets up and goes to the door and back, evidently much preoccupied. SASHA sits down in her former place. IVANOFF silently shakes hands with every one.

LEBEDIEFF. [To SHABELSKI] What miracle has brought you here? You have given us a great surprise. Why, Count, you're a rascal, you haven't been treating us right at all. [Leads him forward by the hand] Tell me, why don't you ever come to see us now? Are you offended?

SHABELSKI. How can I get here to see you? Astride a broomstick? I have no horses of my own, and Nicholas won't take me with him when he goes out. He says I must stay at home to amuse Sarah. Send your horses for me and I shall come with pleasure.

LEBE DIEFF. [With a wave of the hand] Oh, that is easy to say! But Zuzu would rather have a fit than lend the horses to any one. My dear, dear old friend, you are more to me than any one I know! You and I are survivors of those good old days that are gone forever, and you alone bring back to my mind the love and longings of my lost youth. Of course I am only joking, and yet, do you know, I am almost in tears?

SHABELSKI. Stop, stop! You smell like the air of a wine cellar.

LEBEDIEFF. Dear friend, you cannot imagine how lonely I am without my old companions! I could hang myself! [Whispers] Zuzu has frightened all the decent men away with her stingy ways, and now we have only this riff-raff, as you see: Tom, Dick, and Harry. However, drink your tea.

ZINAIDA. [Anxiously, to GABRIEL] Don't bring it in like that! Go fetch some jam to eat with it!

SHABELSKI. [Laughing loudly, to IVANOFF] Didn't I tell you so? [To LEBEDIEFF] I bet him driving over, that as soon as we arrived Zuzu would want to feed us with jam!

ZINAIDA. Still joking, Count! [She sits down.]

LEBEDIEFF. She made twenty jars of it this year, and how else do you expect her to get rid of it?

SHABELSKI. [Sits down near the table] Are you still adding to the hoard, Zuzu? You will soon have a million, eh?

ZINAIDA. [Sighing] I know it seems as if no one could be richer than we, but where do they think the money comes from? It is all gossip.

SHABELSKI. Oh, yes, we all know that! We know how badly you play your cards! Tell me, Paul, honestly, have you saved up a million yet?

LEBEDIEFF. I don't know. Ask Zuzu.

SHABELSKI. [To MARTHA] And my plump little Birdie here will soon have a million too! She is getting prettier and plumper not only every day, but every hour. That means she has a nice little fortune.

MARTHA. Thank you very much, your highness, but I don't like such jokes.

SHABELSKI. My dear little gold mine, do you call that a joke? It was a wail of the soul, a cry from the heart, that burst through my lips. My love for you and Zuzu is immense. [Gaily] Oh, rapture! Oh, bliss! I cannot look at you two without a madly beating heart!

ZINAIDA. You are still the same, Count. [To GEORGE] Put out the candles please, George. [GEORGE gives a start. He puts out the candles and sits down again] How is your wife, Nicholas?

IVANOFF. She is very ill. The doctor said to-day that she certainly had consumption.

ZINAIDA. Really? Oh, how sad! [She sighs] And we are all so fond of her!

SHABELSKI. What trash you all talk! That story was invented by that sham doctor, and is nothing but a trick of his. He wants to masquerade as an Aesculapius, and so has started this consumption theory. Fortunately her husband isn't jealous. [IVANOFF makes an inpatient gesture] As for Sarah, I wouldn't trust a word or an action of hers. I have made a point all my life of mistrusting all doctors, lawyers, and women. They are shammers and deceivers.

LEBEDIEFF. [To SHABELSKI] You are an extraordinary person, Matthew! You have mounted this misanthropic hobby of yours, and you ride it through thick and thin like a lunatic You are a man like any other, and yet, from the way you talk one would imagine that you had the pip, or a cold in the head.

SHABELSKI. Would you have me go about kissing every rascal and scoundrel I meet?

LEBEDIEFF. Where do you find all these rascals and scoundrels?

SHABELSKI. Of course I am not talking of any one here present, nevertheless——

LEBEDIEFF. There you are again with your "nevertheless." All this is simply a fancy of yours.

SHABELSKI. A fancy? It is lucky for you that you have no knowledge of the world!

LEBEDIEFF. My knowledge of the world is this: I must sit here prepared at any moment to have death come knocking at the door. That is my knowledge of the world. At our age, brother, you and I can't afford to worry about knowledge of the world. So then—[He calls] Oh, Gabriel!

SHABELSKI. You have had quite enough already. Look at your nose.

LEBEDIEFF. No matter, old boy. I am not going to be married to-day.

ZINAIDA. Doctor Lvoff has not been here for a long time. He seems to have forgotten us.

SASHA. That man is one of my aversions. I can't stand his icy sense of honour. He can't ask for a glass of water or smoke a cigarette without making a display of his remarkable honesty. Walking and talking, it is written on his brow: "I am an honest man." He is a great bore.

SHABELSKI. He is a narrow-minded, conceited medico. [Angrily] He shrieks like a parrot at every step: "Make way for honest endeavour!" and thinks himself another St. Francis. Everybody is a rascal who doesn't make as much noise as he does. As for his penetration, it is simply remarkable! If a peasant is well off and lives decently, he sees at once that he must be a thief and a scoundrel. If I wear a velvet coat and am dressed by my valet, I am a rascal and the valet is my slave. There is no place in this world for a man like him. I am actually afraid of him. Yes, indeed, he is likely, out of a sense of duty, to insult a man at any moment and to call him a knave.

IVANOFF. I am dreadfully tired of him, but I can't help liking him, too, he is so sincere.

SHABELSKI. Oh, yes, his sincerity is beautiful! He came up to me yesterday evening and remarked absolutely apropos of nothing: "Count, I have a deep aversion to you!" It isn't as if he said such things simply, but they are extremely pointed. His voice trembles, his eyes flash, his veins swell. Confound his infernal honesty! Supposing I am disgusting and odious to him? What is more natural? I know that I am, but I don't like to be told so to my face. I am a worthless old man, but he might have the decency to respect my grey hairs. Oh, what stupid, heartless honesty!

LEBEDIEFF. Come, come, you have been young yourself, and should make allowances for him.

SHABELSKI. Yes, I have been young and reckless; I have played the fool in my day and have seen plenty of knaves and scamps, but I have never called a thief a thief to his face, or talked of ropes in the house of a man who had been hung. I knew how to behave, but this idiotic doctor of yours would think himself in the seventh heaven of happiness if fate would allow him to pull my nose in public in the name of morality and human ideals.

LEBEDIEFF. Young men are all stubborn and restive. I had an uncle once who thought himself a philosopher. He would fill his house with guests, and after he had had a drink he would get up on a chair, like this, and begin: "You ignoramuses! You powers of darkness! This is the dawn of a new life!" And so on and so on; he would preach and preach——

SASHA. And the guests?

LEBEDIEFF. They would just sit and listen and go on drinking. Once, though, I challenged him to a duel, challenged my own uncle! It came out of a discussion about Sir Francis Bacon. I was sitting, I remember, where Matthew is, and my uncle and the late Gerasim Nilitch were standing over there, about where Nicholas is now. Well, Gerasim Nilitch propounded this question——

Enter BORKIN. He is dressed like a dandy and carries a parcel under his arm. He comes in singing and skipping through the door on the right. A murmur of approval is heard.

THE GIRLS. Oh, Michael Borkin!

LEBEDIEFF. Hallo, Misha!

SHABELSKI. The soul of the company!

BORKIN. Here we are! [He runs up to SASHA] Most noble Signorina, let me be so bold as to wish to the whole world many happy returns of the birthday of such an exquisite flower as you! As a token of my enthusiasm let me presume to present you with these fireworks and this Bengal fire of my own manufacture. [He hands her the parcel] May they illuminate the night as brightly as you illuminate the shadows of this dark world. [He spreads them out theatrically before her.]

SASHA. Thank you.

LEBEDIEFF. [Laughing loudly, to IVANOFF] Why don't you send this Judas packing?

BORKIN. [To LEBEDIEFF] My compliments to you, sir. [To IVANOFF] How are you, my patron? [Sings] Nicholas voila, hey ho hey! [He greets everybody in turn] Most highly honoured Zinaida! Oh, glorious Martha! Most ancient Avdotia! Noblest of Counts!

SHABELSKI. [Laughing] The life of the company! The moment he comes in the air feels livelier. Have you noticed it?

BORKIN. Whew! I am tired! I believe I have shaken hands with everybody. Well, ladies and gentlemen, haven't you some little tidbit to tell me; something spicy? [Speaking quickly to ZINAIDA] Oh, aunty! I have something to tell you. As I was on my way here—[To GABRIEL] Some tea, please Gabriel, but without jam—as I was on my way here I saw some peasants down on the river-bank pulling the bark off the trees. Why don't you lease that meadow?

LEBEDIEFF. [To IVANOFF] Why don't you send that Judas away?

ZINAIDA. [Startled] Why, that is quite true! I never thought of it.

BORKIN. [Swinging his arms] I can't sit still! What tricks shall we be up to next, aunty? I am all on edge, Martha, absolutely exalted. [He sings]

"Once more I stand before thee!"

ZINAIDA. Think of something to amuse us, Misha, we are all bored.

BORKIN. Yes, you look so. What is the matter with you all? Why are you sitting there as solemn as a jury? Come, let us play something; what shall it be? Forfeits? Hide-and-seek? Tag? Shall we dance, or have the fireworks?

THE GIRLS. [Clapping their hands] The fireworks! The fireworks! [They run into the garden.]

SASHA. [To IVANOFF] What makes you so depressed today?

IVANOFF. My head aches, little Sasha, and then I feel bored.

SASHA. Come into the sitting-room with me.

They go out through the door on the right. All the guests go into the garden and ZINAIDA and LEBEDIEFF are left alone.

ZINAIDA. That is what I like to see! A young man like Misha comes into the room and in a minute he has everybody laughing. [She puts out the large lamp] There is no reason the candles should burn for nothing so long as they are all in the garden. [She blows out the candles.]

LEBEDIEFF. [Following her] We really ought to give our guests something to eat, Zuzu!

ZINAIDA. What crowds of candles; no wonder we are thought rich.

LEBEDIEFF. [Still following her] Do let them have something to eat, Zuzu; they are young and must be hungry by now, poor things—Zuzu!

ZINAIDA. The Count did not finish his tea, and all that sugar has been wasted. [Goes out through the door on the left.]

LEBEDIEFF. Bah! [Goes out into the garden.]

Enter IVANOFF and SASHA through the door on the right.

IVANOFF. This is how it is, Sasha: I used to work hard and think hard, and never tire; now, I neither do anything nor think anything, and I am weary, body and soul. I feel I am terribly to blame, my conscience leaves me no peace day or night, and yet I can't see clearly exactly what my mistakes are. And now comes my wife's illness, our poverty, this eternal backbiting, gossiping, chattering, that foolish Borkin—My home has become unendurable to me, and to live there is worse than torture. Frankly, Sasha, the presence of my wife, who loves me, has become unbearable. You are an old friend, little

Sasha, you will not be angry with me for speaking so openly. I came to you to be cheered, but I am bored here too, something urges me home again. Forgive me, I shall slip away at once.

SASHA. I can understand your trouble, Nicholas. You are unhappy because you are lonely. You need some one at your side whom you can love, someone who understands you.

IVANOFF. What an idea, Sasha! Fancy a crusty old badger like myself starting a love affair! Heaven preserve me from such misfortune! No, my little sage, this is not a case for romance. The fact is, I can endure all I have to suffer: sadness, sickness of mind, ruin, the loss of my wife, and my lonely, broken old age, but I cannot, I will not, endure the contempt I have for myself! I am nearly killed by shame when I think that a strong, healthy man like myself has become—oh, heaven only knows what—by no means a Manfred or a Hamlet! There are some unfortunates who feel flattered when people call them Hamlets and cynics, but to me it is an insult. It wounds my pride and I am tortured by shame and suffer agony.

SASHA. [Laughing through her tears] Nicholas, let us run away to America together!

IVANOFF. I haven't the energy to take such a step as that, and besides, in America you—[They go toward the door into the garden] As a matter of fact, Sasha, this is not a good place for you to live. When I look about at the men who surround you I am terrified for you; whom is there you could marry? Your only chance will be if some passing lieutenant or student steals your heart and carries you away.

Enter ZINAIDA through the door on the right with a jar of jam.

IVANOFF. Excuse me, Sasha, I shall join you in a minute.

SASHA goes out into the garden.

IVANOFF. [To ZINAIDA] Zinaida, may I ask you a favour?

ZINAIDA. What is it?

IVANOFF. The fact is, you know, that the interest on my note is due day after tomorrow, but I should be more than obliged to you if you will let me postpone the payment of it, or would let me add the interest to the capital. I simply cannot pay it now; I haven't the money.

ZINAIDA. Oh, Ivanoff, how could I do such a thing? Would it be business-like? No, no, don't ask it, don't torment an unfortunate old woman.

IVANOFF. I beg your pardon. [He goes out into the garden.]

ZINAIDA. Oh, dear! Oh, dear! What a fright he gave me! I am trembling all over. [Goes out through the door on the right.]

Enter KOSICH through the door on the left. He walks across the stage.

KOSICH. I had the ace, king, queen, and eight of diamonds, the ace of spades, and one, just one little heart, and she—may the foul fiend fly away with her,—she couldn't make a little slam!

Goes out through the door on the right. Enter from the garden AVDOTIA and FIRST GUEST.

AVDOTIA. Oh, how I should like to get my claws into her, the miserable old miser! How I should like it! Does she think it a joke to leave us sitting here since five o'clock without even offering us a crust to eat? What a house! What management!

FIRST GUEST. I am so bored that I feel like beating my head against the wall. Lord, what a queer lot of people! I shall soon be howling like a wolf and snapping at them from hunger and weariness.

AVDOTIA. How I should like to get my claws into her, the old sinner!

FIRST GUEST. I shall get a drink, old lady, and then home I go! I won't have anything to do with these belles of yours. How the devil can a man think of love who hasn't had a drop to drink since dinner?

AVDOTIA. Come on, we will go and find something.

FIRST GUEST. Sh! Softly! I think the brandy is in the sideboard in the dining-room. We will find George! Sh!

They go out through the door on the left. Enter ANNA and LVOFF through the door on the right.

ANNA. No, they will be glad to see us. Is no one here? Then they must be in the garden.

LVOFF. I should like to know why you have brought me into this den of wolves. This is no place for you and me; honourable people should not be subjected to such influences as these.

ANNA. Listen to me, Mr. Honourable Man. When you are escorting a lady it is very bad manners to talk to her the whole way about nothing but your own honesty. Such behaviour may be perfectly honest, but it is also tedious, to say the least. Never tell a woman how good you are; let her find it out herself. My Nicholas used only to sing and tell stories when he was young as you are, and yet every woman knew at once what kind of a man he was.

LVOFF. Don't talk to me of your Nicholas; I know all about him!

ANNA. You are a very worthy man, but you don't know anything at all. Come into the garden. He never said: "I am an honest man; these surroundings are too narrow for me." He never spoke of wolves' dens, called people bears or vultures. He left the animal kingdom alone, and the most I have ever heard him say when he was excited was: "Oh, how unjust I have been to-day!" or "Annie, I am sorry for that man." That's what he would say, but you—

ANNA and LVOFF go out. Enter AVDOTIA and FIRST GUEST through the door on the left.

FIRST GUEST. There isn't any in the dining-room, so it must be somewhere in the pantry. We must find George. Come this way, through the sitting-room.

AVDOTIA. Oh, how I should like to get my claws into her!

They go out through the door on the right. MARTHA and BORKIN run in laughing from the garden. SHABELSK I comes mincing behind them, laughing and rubbing his hands.

MARTHA. Oh, I am so bored! [Laughs loudly] This is deadly! Every one looks as if he had swallowed a poker. I am frozen to the marrow by this icy dullness. [She skips about] Let us do something!

BORKIN catches her by the waist and kisses her cheek.

SHABELSKI. [Laughing and snapping his fingers] Well, I'll be hanged! [Cackling] Really, you know!

MARTHA. Let go! Let go, you wretch! What will the Count think? Stop, I say!

BORKIN. Angel! Jewel! Lend me twenty-three hundred roubles.

MARTHA. Most certainly not! Do what you please, but I'll thank you to leave my money alone. No, no, no! Oh, let go, will you?

SHABELSKI. [Mincing around them] The little birdie has its charms! [Seriously] Come, that will do!

BORKIN. Let us come to the point, and consider my proposition frankly as a business arrangement. Answer me honestly, without tricks and equivocations, do you agree to do it or not? Listen to me; [Pointing to Shabelski] he needs money to the amount of at least three thousand a year; you need a husband. Do you want to be a Countess?

SHABELSKI. [Laughing loudly] Oh, the cynic!

BORKIN. Do you want to be a Countess or not?

MARTHA. [Excitedly] Wait a minute; really, Misha, these things aren't done in a second like this. If the Count wants to marry me, let him ask me himself, and—and—I don't see, I don't understand—all this is so sudden——

BORKIN. Come, don't let us beat about the bush; this is a business arrangement. Do you agree or not?

SHABELSKI. [Chuckling and rubbing his hands] Supposing I do marry her, eh? Hang it, why shouldn't I play her this shabby trick? What do you say, little puss? [He kisses her cheek] Dearest chick-a-biddy!

MARTHA. Stop! Stop! I hardly know what I am doing. Go away! No—don't go!

BORKIN. Answer at once: is it yes or no? We can't stand here forever.

MARTHA. Look here, Count, come and visit me for three or four days. It is gay at my house, not like this place. Come to-morrow. [To BORKIN] Or is this all a joke?

BORKIN. [Angrily] How could I joke on such a serious subject?

MARTHA. Wait! Stop! Oh, I feel faint! A Countess! I am fainting, I am falling!

BORKIN and SHABELSKI laugh and catch her by the arms. They kiss her cheeks and lead her out through the door on the right. IVANOFF and SASHA run in from the garden.

IVANOFF. [Desperately clutching his head] It can't be true! Don't Sasha, don't! Oh, I implore you not to!

SASHA. I love you madly. Without you my life can have no meaning, no happiness, no hope.

IVANOFF. Why, why do you say that? What do you mean? Little Sasha, don't say it!

SASHA. You were the only joy of my childhood; I loved you body and soul then, as myself, but now—Oh, I love you, Nicholas! Take me with you to the ends of the earth, wherever you wish; but for heaven's sake let us go at once, or I shall die.

IVANOFF. [Shaking with wild laughter] What is this? Is it the beginning for me of a new life? Is it, Sasha? Oh, my happiness, my joy! [He draws her to him] My freshness, my youth!

Enter ANNA from the garden. She sees her husband and SASHA, and stops as if petrified.

IVANOFF. Oh, then I shall live once more? And work?

IVANOFF and SASHA kiss each other. After the kiss they look around and see ANNA.

IVANOFF. [With horror] Sarah!

The curtain falls.

ACT III

Library in IVANOFF'S house. On the walls hang maps, pictures, guns, pistols, sickles, whips, etc. A writing-table. On it lie in disorder knick-knacks, papers, books, parcels, and several revolvers. Near the papers stand a lamp, a decanter of vodka, and a plate of salted herrings. Pieces of bread and cucumber are scattered about. SHABELSKI and LEBEDIEFF are sitting at the writing-table. BORKIN is sitting astride a chair in the middle of the room. PETER is standing near the door.

LEBEDIEFF. The policy of France is clear and definite; the French know what they want: it is to skin those German sausages, but the Germans must sing another song; France is not the only thorn in their flesh.

SHABELSKI. Nonsense! In my opinion the Germans are cowards and the French are the same. They are showing their teeth at one another, but you can take my word for it, they will not do more than that; they'll never fight!

BORKIN. Why should they fight? Why all these congresses, this arming and expense? Do you know what I would do in their place? I would catch all the dogs in the kingdom and inoculate them with Pasteur's serum, then I would let them loose in the enemy's country, and the enemies would all go mad in a month.

LEBEDIEFF. [Laughing] His head is small, but the great ideas are hidden away in it like fish in the sea!

SHABELSKI. Oh, he is a genius.

LEBEDIEFF. Heaven help you, Misha, you are a funny chap. [He stops laughing] But how is this, gentlemen? Here we are talking Germany, Germany, and never a word about vodka! Repetatur! [He fills three glasses] Here's to you all! [He drinks and eats] This herring is the best of all relishes.

SHABELSKI. No, no, these cucumbers are better; every wise man since the creation of the world has been trying to invent something better than a salted cucumber, and not one has succeeded. [To PETER] Peter, go and fetch some more cucumbers. And Peter, tell the cook to make four little onion pasties, and see that we get them hot.

PETER goes out.

LEBEDIEFF. Caviar is good with vodka, but it must be prepared with skill. Take a quarter of a pound of pressed caviar, two little onions, and a little olive oil; mix them together and put a slice of lemon on top—so! Lord! The very perfume would drive you crazy!

BORKIN. Roast snipe are good too, but they must be cooked right. They should first be cleaned, then sprinkled with bread crumbs, and roasted until they will crackle between the teeth—crunch, crunch!

SHABELSKI. We had something good at Martha's yesterday: white mushrooms.

LEBEDIEFF. You don't say so!

SHABELSKI. And they were especially well prepared, too, with onions and bay-leaves and spices, you know. When the dish was opened, the odour that floated out was simply intoxicating!

LEBEDIEFF. What do you say, gentlemen? Repetatur! [He drinks] Good health to you! [He looks at his watch] I must be going. I can't wait for Nicholas. So you say Martha gave you mushrooms? We haven't seen one at home. Will you please tell me, Count, what plot you are hatching that takes you to Martha's so often?

SHABELSKI. [Nodding at BORKIN] He wants me to marry her.

LEBEDIEFF. Wants you to marry her! How old are you?

SHABELSKI. Sixty-two.

LEBEDIEFF. Really, you are just the age to marry, aren't you? And Martha is just suited to you!

BORKIN. This is not a question of Martha, but of Martha's money.

LEBEDIEFF. Aren't you moonstruck, and don't you want the moon too?

SHABELSKI. Borkin here is quite in earnest about it; the clever fellow is sure I shall obey orders, and marry Martha.

BORKIN. What do you mean? Aren't you sure yourself?

SHABELSKI. Are you mad? I never was sure of anything. Bah!

BORKIN. Many thanks! I am much obliged to you for the information. So you are trying to fool me, are you? First you say you will marry Martha and then you say you won't; the devil only knows which you really mean, but I have given her my word of honour that you will. So you have changed your mind, have you?

SHABELSKI. He is actually in earnest; what an extraordinary man!

BORKIN. [losing his temper] If that is how you feel about it, why have you turned an honest woman's head? Her heart is set on your title, and she can neither eat nor sleep for thinking of it. How can you make a jest of such things? Do you think such behaviour is honourable?

SHABELSKI. [Snapping his fingers] Well, why not play her this shabby trick, after all? Eh? Just out of spite? I shall certainly do it, upon my word I shall! What a joke it will be!

Enter LVOFF.

LEBEDIEFF. We bow before you, Aesculapius! [He shakes hands with LVOFF and sings]

```
"Doctor, doctor, save, oh, save me,
 I am scared to death of dying!"
```

LVOFF. Hasn't Ivanoff come home yet?

LEBEDIEFF. Not yet. I have been waiting for him myself for over an hour.

LVOFF walks impatiently up and down.

LEBEDIEFF. How is Anna to-day?

LVOFF. Very ill.

LEBEDIEFF. [Sighing] May one go and pay one's respects to her?

LVOFF. No, please don't. She is asleep, I believe.

LEBEDIEFF. She is a lovely, charming woman. [Sighing] The day she fainted at our house, on Sasha's birthday, I saw that she had not much longer to live, poor thing. Let me see, why did she faint? When I ran up, she was lying on the floor, ashy white, with Nicholas on his knees beside her, and Sasha was standing by them in tears. Sasha and I went about almost crazy for a week after that.

SHABELSKI. [To LVOFF] Tell me, most honoured disciple of science, what scholar discovered that the frequent visits of a young doctor were beneficial to ladies suffering from affections of the chest? It is a remarkable discovery, remarkable! Would you call such treatment Allopathic or Homeopathic?

LVOFF tries to answer, but makes an impatient gesture instead, and walks out of the room.

SHABELSKI. What a withering look he gave me!

LEBEDIEFF. Some fiend must prompt you to say such things! Why did you offend him?

SHABELSKI. [Angrily] Why does he tell such lies? Consumption! No hope! She is dying! It is nonsense, I can't abide him!

LEBEDIEFF. What makes you think he is lying?

SHABELSKI. [Gets up and walks up and down] I can't bear to think that a living person could die like that, suddenly, without any reason at all. Don't let us talk about it!

KOSICH runs in panting.

KOSICH. Is Ivanoff at home? How do you do? [He shakes hands quickly all round] Is he at home?

BORKIN. No, he isn't.

KOSICH. [Sits down and jumps up again] In that case I must say goodbye; I must be going. Business, you know. I am absolutely exhausted; run off my feet!

LEBEDIEFF. Where did you blow in from?

KOSICH. From Barabanoff's. He and I have been playing cards all night; we have only just stopped. I have been absolutely fleeced; that Barabanoff is a demon at cards. [In a tearful voice] Just listen to this: I had a heart and he [He turns to BORKIN, who jumps away from him] led a diamond, and I led a heart, and he led another diamond. Well, he didn't take the trick. [To LEBEDIEFF] We were playing three in clubs. I had the ace and queen, and the ace and ten of spades—

LEBEDIEFF. [Stopping up his ears] Spare me, for heaven's sake, spare me!

KOSICH. [To SHABELSKI] Do you understand? I had the ace and queen of clubs, the ace and ten of spades.

SHABELSKI. [Pushes him away] Go away, I don't want to listen to you!

KOSICH. When suddenly misfortune overtook me. My ace of spades took the first trick—

SHABELSKI. [Snatching up a revolver] Leave the room, or I shall shoot!

KOSICH. [Waving his hands] What does this mean? Is this the Australian bush, where no one has any interests in common? Where there is no public spirit, and each man lives for himself alone? However, I must be off. My time is precious. [He shakes hands with LEBEDIEFF] Pass!

General laughter. KOSICH goes out. In the doorway he runs into AVDOTIA.

AVDOTIA. [Shrieks] Bad luck to you, you nearly knocked me down.

ALL. Oh, she is always everywhere at once!

AVDOTIA. So this is where you all are? I have been looking for you all over the house. Good-day to you, boys!

[She shakes hands with everybody.]

LEBEDIEFF. What brings you here?

AVDOTIA. Business, my son. [To SHABELSKI] Business connected with your highness. She commanded me to bow. [She bows] And to inquire after your health. She told me to say, the little birdie, that if you did not come to see her this evening she would cry her eyes out. Take him aside, she said, and whisper in his ear. But why should I make a secret of her message? We are not stealing chickens, but arranging an affair of lawful love by mutual consent of both parties. And now, although I never drink, I shall take a drop under these circumstances.

LEBEDIEFF. So shall I. [He pours out the vodka] You must be immortal, you old magpie! You were an old woman when I first knew you, thirty years ago.

AVDOTIA. I have lost count of the years. I have buried three husbands, and would have married a fourth if any one had wanted a woman without a dowry. I have had eight children. [She takes up the glass] Well, we have begun a good work, may it come to a good end! They will live happily ever after, and we shall enjoy their happiness. Love and good luck to them both! [She drinks] This is strong vodka!

SHABELSKI. [laughing loudly, to LEBEDIEFF] The funny thing is, they actually think I am in earnest. How strange! [He gets up] And yet, Paul, why shouldn't I play her this shabby trick? Just out of spite? To give the devil something to do, eh, Paul?

LEBEDIEFF. You are talking nonsense, Count. You and I must fix our thoughts on dying now; we have left Martha's money far behind us; our day is over.

SHABELSKI. No, I shall certainly marry her; upon my word, I shall!

Enter IVANOFF and LVOFF.

LVOFF. Will you please spare me five minutes of your time?

LEBEDIEFF. Hallo, Nicholas! [He goes to meet IVANOFF] How are you, old friend? I have been waiting an hour for you.

AVDOTIA. [Bows] How do you do, my son?

IVANOFF. [Bitterly] So you have turned my library into a bar-room again, have you? And yet I have begged you all a thousand times not to do so! [He goes up to the table] There, you see, you have spilt vodka all over my papers and scattered crumbs and cucumbers everywhere! It is disgusting!

LEBEDIEFF. I beg your pardon, Nicholas. Please forgive me. I have something very important to speak to you about.

BORKIN. So have I.

LVOFF. May I have a word with you?

IVANOFF. [Pointing to LEBEDIEFF] He wants to speak to me; wait a minute. [To LEBEDIEFF] Well, what is it?

LEBEDIEFF. [To the others] Excuse me, ladies and gentlemen, I want to speak to him in private.

SHABELSKI goes out, followed by AVDOTIA, BORKIN, and LVOFF.

IVANOFF. Paul, you may drink yourself as much as you choose, it is your weakness, but I must ask you not to make my uncle tipsy. He never used to drink at all; it is bad for him.

LEBEDIEFF. [Startled] My dear boy, I didn't know that! I wasn't thinking of him at all.

IVANOFF. If this old baby should die on my hands the blame would be mine, not yours. Now, what do you want? [A pause.]

LEBEDIEFF. The fact is, Nicholas—I really don't know how I can put it to make it seem less brutal—Nicholas, I am ashamed of myself, I am blushing, my tongue sticks to the roof of my mouth. My dear boy, put yourself in my place; remember that I am not a free man, I am as putty in the hands of my wife, a slave—forgive me!

IVANOFF. What does this mean?

LEBEDIEFF. My wife has sent me to you; do me a favour, be a friend to me, pay her the interest on the money you owe her. Believe me, she has been tormenting me and going for me tooth and nail. For heaven's sake, free yourself from her clutches!

IVANOFF. You know, Paul, that I have no money now.

LEBEDIEFF. I know, I know, but what can I do? She won't wait. If she should sue you for the money, how could Sasha and I ever look you in the face again?

IVANOFF. I am ready to sink through the floor with shame, Paul, but where, where shall I get the money? Tell me, where? There is nothing I can do but to wait until I sell my wheat in the autumn.

LEBEDIEFF. [Shrieks] But she won't wait! [A pause.]

IVANOFF. Your position is very delicate and unpleasant, but mine is even worse. [He walks up and down in deep thought] I am at my wit's end, there is nothing I can sell now.

LEBEDIEFF. You might go to Mulbach and get some money from him; doesn't he owe you sixty thousand roubles?

IVANOFF makes a despairing gesture.

LEBEDIEFF. Listen to me, Nicholas, I know you will be angry, but you must forgive an old drunkard like me. This is between friends; remember I am your friend. We were students together, both Liberals; we had the same interests and ideals; we studied together at the University of Moscow. It is our Alma Mater. [He takes out his purse] I have a private fund here; not a soul at home knows of its existence. Let me lend it to you. [He takes out the money and lays it on the table] Forget your pride; this is between friends! I should take it from you, indeed I should! [A pause] There is the money, one hundred thousand roubles. Take it; go to her y ourself and say: "Take the money,

Zinaida, and may you choke on it." Only, for heaven's sake, don't let her see by your manner that you got it from me, or she would certainly go for me, with her old jam! [He looks intently into IVANOFF'S face] There, there, no matter. [He quickly takes up the money and stuffs it back into his pocket] Don't take it, I was only joking. Forgive me! Are you hurt?

IVANOFF waves his hand.

LEBEDIEFF. Yes, the truth is—[He sighs] This is a time of sorrow and pain for you. A man, brother, is like a samovar; he cannot always stand coolly on a shelf; hot coals will be dropped into him some day, and then—fizz! The comparison is idiotic, but it is the best I can think of. [Sighing] Misfortunes wring the soul, and yet I am not worried about you, brother. Wheat goes through the mill, and comes out as flour, and you will come safely through your troubles; but I am annoyed, Nicholas, and angry with the people around you. The whole countryside is buzzing with gossip; where does it all start? They say you will be soon arrested for your debts, that you are a bloodthirsty murderer, a monster of cruelty, a robber.

IVANOFF. All that is nothing to me; my head is aching.

LEBEDIEFF. Because you think so much.

IVANOFF. I never think.

LEBEDIEFF. Come, Nicholas, snap your fingers at the whole thing, and drive over to visit us. Sasha loves and understands you. She is a sweet, honest, lovely girl; too good to be the child of her mother and me! Sometimes, when I look at her, I cannot believe that such a treasure could belong to a fat old drunkard like me. Go to her, talk to her, and let her cheer you. She is a good, true-hearted girl.

IVANOFF. Paul, my dear friend, please go, and leave me alone.

LEBEDIEFF. I understand, I understand! [He glances at his watch] Yes, I understand. [He kisses IVANOFF] Good-bye, I must go to the blessing of the school now. [He goes as far as the door, then stops] She is so clever! Sasha and I were talking about gossiping yesterday, and she flashed out this epigram: "Father," she said, "fire-flies shine at night so that the night-birds may make them their prey, and good people are made to be preyed upon by gossips and slanderers." What do you think of that? She is a genius, another George Sand!

IVANOFF. [Stopping him as he goes out] Paul, what is the matter with me?

LEBEDIEFF. I have wanted to ask you that myself, but I must confess I was ashamed to. I don't know, old chap. Sometimes I think your troubles have been too heavy for you, and yet I know you are not the kind to give in to them; you would not be overcome by misfortune. It must be something else, Nicholas, but what it may be I can't imagine.

IVANOFF. I can't imagine either what the matter is, unless—and yet no—[A pause] Well, do you see, this is what I wanted to say. I used to have a workman called Simon, you remember him. Once, at threshing-time, to show the girls how strong he was, he loaded himself with two sacks of rye, and broke his back. He died soon after. I think I have broken my back also. First I went to school, then to the university, then came the cares of this estate, all my plans—I did not believe what others did; did not marry as others did; I worked passionately, risked everything; no one else, as you know, threw their money away to right and left as I did. So I heaped the burdens on my back, and it broke. We are all heroes at twenty, ready to attack anything, to do everything, and at thirty are worn-out, useless men. How, oh, how do you account for this weariness? However, I may be quite wrong; go away, Paul, I am boring you.

LEBEDIEFF. I know what is the matter with you, old man: you got out of bed on the wrong side this morning.

IVANOFF. That is stupid, Paul, and stale. Go away!

LEBEDIEFF. It is stupid, certainly. I see that myself now. I am going at once. [LEBEDIEFF goes out.]

IVANOFF. [Alone] I am a worthless, miserable, useless man. Only a man equally miserable and suffering, as Paul is, could love or esteem me now. Good God! How I loathe myself! How bitterly I hate my voice, my hands, my thoughts, these clothes, each step I take! How ridiculous it is, how disgusting! Less than a year ago I was healthy and strong, full of pride and energy and enthusiasm. I worked with these hands here, and my words could move the dullest man to tears. I could weep with sorrow, and grow indignant at the sight of wrong. I could feel the glow of inspiration, and understand the beauty and romance of the silent nights which I used to watch through from evening until dawn, sitting at my worktable, and giving up my soul to dreams. I believed in a bright future then, and looked into it as trustfully as a child looks into its mother's eyes. And now, oh, it is terrible! I am tired and without hope; I spend my days and nights in idleness; I have no control over my feet or brain. My estate is ruined, my woods are falling under the blows of the axe. [He weeps] My neglected land looks up at me as reproachfully as an orphan. I expect nothing, am sorry for nothing; my whole soul trembles at the thought of each new day. And what can I think of my treatment of Sarah? I promised her love and happiness forever; I opened her eyes to the promise of a future such as she had never even dreamed of. She believed me, and though for five years I have seen her sinking under the weight of her sacrifices to me, and losing her strength in her struggles with her conscience, God knows she has never given me one angry look, or uttered one word of reproach. What is the result? That I don't love her! Why? Is it possible? Can it be true? I can't understand. She is suffering; her days are numbered; yet I fly like a contemptible coward from her white face, her sunken chest, her pleading eyes. Oh, I am ashamed, ashamed! [A pause] Sasha, a young girl, is sorry for me in my misery. She confesses to me that she loves me; me, almost an old man! Whereupon I lose my head, and exalted as if by music, I yell: "Hurrah for a new life and new happiness!" Next day I believe in this new life and happiness as little as I believe in my happiness at home. What is the matter with me? What is this pit I am wallowing in? What is the cause of this weakness? What does this nervousness come from? If my sick wife wounds my pride, if a servant makes a mistake, if my gun misses fire, I lose my temper and get violent and altogether unlike myself. I can't, I can't understand it; the easiest way out would be a bullet through the head!

Enter LVOFF.

LVOFF. I must have an explanation with you, Ivanoff.

IVANOFF. If we are going to have an explanation every day, doctor, we shall neither of us have the strength to stand it.

LVOFF. Will you be good enough to hear me?

IVANOFF. I have heard all you have told me every day, and have failed to discover yet what you want me to do.

LVOFF. I have always spoken plainly enough, and only an utterly heartless and cruel man could fail to understand me.

IVANOFF. I know that my wife is dying; I know that I have sinned irreparably; I know that you are an honest man. What more can you tell me?

LVOFF. The sight of human cruelty maddens me. The woman is dying and she has a mother and father whom she loves, and longs to see once more before she dies. They know that she is dying and that she loves them still, but with diabolical cruelty, as if to flaunt their religious zeal, they refuse to see her and forgive her. You are the man for whom she has sacrificed her home, her peace of mind, everything. Yet you unblushingly go gadding to the Lebedieffs' every evening, for reasons that are absolutely unmistakable!

IVANOFF. Ah me, it is two weeks since I was there!

LVOFF. [Not listening to him] To men like yourself one must speak plainly, and if you don't want to hear what I have to say, you need not listen. I always call a spade a spade; the truth is, you want her to die so that the way may be cleared for your other schemes. Be it so; but can't you wait? If, instead of crushing the life out of your wife by your heartless egoism, you let her die naturally, do you think you would lose Sasha and Sasha's money? Such an absolute Tartuffe as you are could turn the girl's head and get her money a year from now as easily as you can to-day. Why are you in such a hurry? Why do you want your wife to die now, instead of in a month's time, or a year's?

IVANOFF. This is torture! You are a very bad doctor if you think a man can control himself forever. It is all I can do not to answer your insults.

LVOFF. Look here, whom are you trying to deceive? Throw off this disguise!

IVANOFF. You who are so clever, you think that nothing in the world is easier than to understand me, do you? I married Annie for her money, did I? And when her parents wouldn't give it to me, I changed my plans, and am now hustling her out of the world so that I may marry another woman, who will bring me what I want? You think so, do you? Oh, how easy and simple it all is! But you are mistaken, doctor; in each one of us there are too many springs, too many wheels and cogs for us to judge each other by first impressions or by two or three external indications. I can not understand you, you cannot understand me, and neither of us can understand himself. A man may be a splendid doctor, and at the same time a very bad judge of human nature; you will admit that, unless you are too self-confident.

LVOFF. Do you really think that your character is so mysterious, and that I am too stupid to tell vice from virtue?

IVANOFF. It is clear that we shall never agree, so let me beg you to answer me now without any more preamble: exactly what do you want me to do? [Angrily] What are you after anyway? And with whom have I the honour of speaking? With my lawyer, or with my wife's doctor?

LVOFF. I am a doctor, and as such I demand that you change your conduct toward your wife; it is killing her.

IVANOFF. What shall I do? Tell me! If you understand me so much better than I understand myself, for heaven's sake tell me exactly what to do!

LVOFF. In the first place, don't be so unguarded in your behaviour.

IVANOFF. Heaven help me, do you mean to say that you understand yourself? [He drinks some water] Now go away; I am guilty a thousand times over; I shall answer for my sins before God; but nothing has given you the right to torture me daily as you do.

LVOFF. Who has given you the right to insult my sense of honour? You have maddened and poisoned my soul. Before I came to this place I knew that stupid, crazy, deluded people existed, but I never imagined that any one could be so criminal as to turn his mind deliberately in the direction of wickedness. I loved and esteemed humanity then, but since I have known you—

IVANOFF. I have heard all that before.

LVOFF. You have, have you?

He goes out, shrugging his shoulders. He sees SASHA, who comes in at this moment dressed for riding.

LVOFF. Now, however, I hope that we can understand one another!

IVANOFF. [Startled] Oh, Sasha, is that you?

SASHA. Yes, it is I. How are you? You didn't expect me, did you? Why haven't you been to see us?

IVANOFF. Sasha, this is really imprudent of you! Your coming will have a terrible effect on my wife!

SASHA. She won't see me; I came in by the back entrance; I shall go in a minute. I am so anxious about you. Tell me, are you well? Why haven't you been to see us for such a long time?

IVANOFF. My wife is offended already, and almost dying, and now you come here; Sasha, Sasha, this is thoughtless and unkind of you.

SASHA. How could I help coming? It is two weeks since you were at our house, and you have not answered my letters. I imagined you suffering dreadfully, or ill, or dead. I have not slept for nights. I am going now, but first tell me that you are well.

IVANOFF. No, I am not well. I am a torment to myself, and every one torments me without end. I can't stand it! And now you come here. How morbid and unnatural it all is, Sasha. I am terribly guilty.

SASHA. What dreadful, pitiful speeches you make! So you are guilty, are you? Tell me, then, what is it you have done?

IVANOFF I don't know; I don't know!

SASHA. That is no answer. Every sinner should know what he is guilty of. Perhaps you have been forging money?

IVANOFF. That is stupid.

SASHA. Or are you guilty because you no longer love your wife? Perhaps you are, but no one is master of his feelings, and you did not mean to stop loving her. Do you feel guilty because she saw me telling you that I love you? No, that cannot be, because you did not want her to see it—

IVANOFF. [Interrupting her] And so on, and so on! First you say I love, and then you say I don't; that I am not master of my feelings. All these are commonplace, worn-out sentiments, with which you cannot help me.

SASHA. It is impossible to talk to you. [She looks at a picture on the wall] How well those dogs are drawn! Were they done from life?

IVANOFF. Yes, from life. And this whole romance of ours is a tedious old story; a man loses heart and begins to go down in the world; a girl appears, brave and strong of heart, and gives him a hand to help him to rise again. Such situations are pretty, but they are only found in novels and not in real life.

SASHA. No, they are found in real life too.

IVANOFF. Now I see how well you understand real life! My sufferings seem noble to you; you imagine you have discovered in me a second Hamlet; but my state of mind in all its phases is only fit to furnish food for contempt and derision. My contortions are ridiculous enough to make any one die of laughter, and you want to play the guardian angel; you want to do a noble deed and save me. Oh, how I hate myself to-day! I feel that this tension must soon be relieved in some way. Either I shall break something, or else—

SASHA. That is exactly what you need. Let yourself go! Smash something; break it to pieces; give a yell! You are angry with me, it was foolish of me to come here. Very well, then, get excited about it; storm at me; stamp your feet! Well, aren't you getting angry?

IVANOFF. You ridiculous girl!

SASHA. Splendid! So we are smiling at last! Be kind, do me the favour of smiling once more!

IVANOFF. [Laughing] I have noticed that whenever you start reforming me and saving my soul, and teaching me how to be good, your face grows naive, oh so naive, and your eyes grow as wide as if you were looking at a comet. Wait a moment; your shoulder is covered with dust. [He brushes her shoulder] A naive man is nothing better than a fool, but you women contrive to be naive in such a way that in you it seems sweet, and gentle, and proper, and not as silly as it really is. What a strange way you have, though, of ignoring a man as long as he is well and happy, and fastening yourselves to him as soon as he begins to whine and go down-hill! Do you actually think it is worse to be the wife of a strong man than to nurse some whimpering invalid?

SASHA. Yes, it is worse.

IVANOFF. Why do you think so? [Laughing loudly] It is a good thing Darwin can't hear what you are saying! He would be furious with you for degrading the human race. Soon, thanks to your kindness, only invalids and hypochondriacs will be born into the world.

SASHA. There are a great many things a man cannot understand. Any girl would rather love an unfortunate man than a fortunate one, because every girl would like to do something by loving. A man has his work to do, and so for him love is kept in the background. To talk to his wife, to walk with her in the garden, to pass the time pleasantly with her, that is all that love means to a man. But for us, love means life. I love you; that means that I dream only of how I shall cure you of your sadness, how I shall go with you to the ends of the earth. If you are in heaven, I am in heaven; if you are in the pit, I am in the pit. For instance, it would be the greatest happiness for me to write all night for you, or to watch all night that no one should wake you. I remember that three years ago, at threshing time, you came to us all dusty and sunburnt and tired, and asked for a drink. When I brought you a glass of water you were already lying on the sofa and sleeping like a dead man. You slept there for half a day, and all that time I watched by the door that no one should disturb you. How happy I was! The more a girl can do, the greater her love will be; that is, I mean, the more she feels it.

IVANOFF. The love that accomplishes things—hm—that is a fairy tale, a girl's dream; and yet, perhaps it is as it should be. [He shrugs his shoulders] How can I tell? [Gaily] On my honour, Sasha, I really am quite a respectable man. Judge for yourself: I have always liked to discuss things, but I have never in my life said that our women were corrupt, or that such and such a woman was on the down-hill path. I have always been grateful, and nothing more. No, nothing more. Dear child, how comical you are! And what a ridiculous old stupid I am! I shock all good Christian folk, and go about complaining from morning to night. [He laughs and then leaves her suddenly] But you must go, Sasha; we have forgotten ourselves.

SASHA. Yes, it is time to go. Good-bye. I am afraid that that honest doctor of yours will have told Anna out of a sense of duty that I am here. Take my advice: go at once to your wife and stay with her. Stay, and stay, and stay, and if it should be for a year, you must still stay, or for ten years. It is your duty. You must repent, and ask her forgiveness, and weep. That is what you ought to do, and the great thing is not to forget to do right.

IVANOFF. Again I feel as if I were going crazy; again!

SASHA. Well, heaven help you! You must forget me entirely. In two weeks you must send me a line and I shall be content with that. But I shall write to you—

BORKIN looks in at the door.

BORKIN. Ivanoff, may I come in? [He sees SASHA] I beg your pardon, I did not see you. Bonjour! [He bows.]

SASHA. [Embarrassed] How do you do?

BORKIN. You are plumper and prettier than ever.

SASHA. [To IVANOFF] I must go, Nicholas, I must go. [She goes out.]

BORKIN. What a beautiful apparition! I came expecting prose and found poetry instead. [Sings]

"You showed yourself to the world as a bird——"

IVANOFF walks excitedly up and down.

BORKIN. [Sits down] There is something in her, Nicholas, that one doesn't find in other women, isn't there? An elfin strangeness. [He sighs] Although she is without doubt the richest girl in the country, her mother is so stingy that no one will have her. After her mother's death Sasha will have the whole fortune, but until then she will only give her ten thousand roubles and an old flat-iron, and to get that she will have to humble herself to the ground. [He feels in his pockets] Will you have a smoke? [He offers IVANOFF his cigarette case] These are very good.

IVANOFF. [Comes toward BORKIN stifled with rage] Leave my house this instant, and don't you ever dare to set foot in it again! Go this instant!

BORKIN gets up and drops his cigarette.

IVANOFF. Go at once!

BORKIN. Nicholas, what do you mean? Why are you so angry?

IVANOFF. Why! Where did you get those cigarettes? Where? You think perhaps that I don't know where you take the old man every day, and for what purpose?

BORKIN. [Shrugs his shoulders] What business is it of yours?

IVANOFF. You blackguard, you! The disgraceful rumours that you have been spreading about me have made me disreputable in the eyes of the whole countryside. You and I have nothing in common, and I ask you to leave my house this instant.

BORKIN. I know that you are saying all this in a moment of irritation, and so I am not angry with you. Insult me as much as you please. [He picks up his cigarette] It is time though, to shake off this melancholy of yours; you're not a schoolboy.

IVANOFF. What did I tell you? [Shuddering] Are you making fun of me?

Enter ANNA.

BORKIN. There now, there comes Anna! I shall go.

IVANOFF stops near the table and stands with his head bowed.

ANNA. [After a pause] What did she come here for? What did she come here for, I ask you?

IVANOFF. Don't ask me, Annie. [A pause] I am terribly guilty. Think of any punishment you want to inflict on me; I can stand anything, but don't, oh, don't ask questions!

ANNA. [Angrily] So that is the sort of man you are? Now I understand you, and can see how degraded, how dishonourable you are! Do you remember that you came to me once and lied to me about your love? I believed you, and left my mother, my father, and my faith to follow you. Yes, you lied to me of goodness and honour, of your noble aspirations and I believed every word——

IVANOFF. I have never lied to you, Annie.

ANNA. I have lived with you five years now, and I am tired and ill, but I have always loved you and have never left you for a moment. You have been my idol, and what have you done? All this time you have been deceiving me in the most dastardly way——

IVANOFF. Annie, don't say what isn't so. I have made mistakes, but I have never told a lie in my life. You dare not accuse me of that!

ANNA. It is all clear to me now. You married me because you expected my mother and father to forgive me and give you my money; that is what you expected.

IVANOFF. Good Lord, Annie! If I must suffer like this, I must have the patience to bear it. [He begins to weep.]

ANNA. Be quiet! When you found that I wasn't bringing you any money, you tried another game. Now I remember and understand everything. [She begins to cry] You have never loved me or been faithful to me—never!

IVANOFF. Sarah! That is a lie! Say what you want, but don't insult me with a lie!

ANNA. You dishonest, degraded man! You owe money to Lebedieff, and now, to escape paying your debts, you are trying to turn the head of his daughter and betray her as you have betrayed me. Can you deny it?

IVANOFF. [Stifled with rage] For heaven's sake, be quiet! I can't answer for what I may do! I am choking with rage and I—I might insult you!

ANNA. I am not the only one whom you have basely deceived. You have always blamed Borkin for all your dishonest tricks, but now I know whose they are.

IVANOFF. Sarah, stop at once and go away, or else I shall say something terrible. I long to say a dreadful, cruel thing [He shrieks] Hold your tongue, Jewess!

ANNA. I won't hold my tongue! You have deceived me too long for me to be silent now.

IVANOFF. So you won't be quiet? [He struggles with himself] Go, for heaven's sake!

ANNA. Go now, and betray Sasha!

IVANOFF. Know then that you—are dying! The doctor told me that you are dying.

ANNA. [Sits down and speaks in a low voice] When did he

IVANOFF. [Clutches his head with both hands] Oh, how guilty I am—how guilty! [He sobs.]

The curtain falls.

About a year passes between the third and fourth acts.

ACT IV

A sitting-room in LEBEDIEFF'S house. In the middle of the wall at the back of the room is an arch dividing the sitting-room from the ballroom. To the right and left are doors. Some old bronzes are placed about the room; family portraits are hanging on the walls. Everything is arranged as if for some festivity. On the piano lies a violin; near it stands a violoncello. During the entire act guests, dressed as for a ball, are seen walking about in the ball-room.

Enter LVOFF, looking at his watch.

LVOFF. It is five o'clock. The ceremony must have begun. First the priest will bless them, and then they will be led to the church to be married. Is this how virtue and justice triumph? Not being able to rob Sarah, he has tortured her to death; and now he has found another victim whom he will deceive until he has robbed her, and then he will get rid of her as he got rid of poor Sarah. It is the same old sordid story. [A pause] He will live to a fine old age in the seventh heaven of happiness, and will die with a clear conscience. No, Ivanoff, it shall not be! I shall drag your villainy to light! And when I tear off that accursed mask of yours and show you to the world as the blackguard you are, you shall come plunging down headfirst from your seventh heaven, into a pit so deep that the devil himself will not be able to drag you out of it! I am a man of honour; it is my duty to interfere in such cases as yours, and to open the eyes of the blind. I shall fulfil my mission, and to-morrow will find me far away from this accursed place. [Thoughtfully] But what shall I do? To have an explanation with Lebedieff would be a hopeless task. Shall I make a scandal, and challenge Ivanoff to a duel? I am as excited as a child, and have entirely lost the power of planning anything. What shall I do? Shall I fight a duel?

Enter KOSICH. He goes gaily up to LVOFF.

KOSICH. I declared a little slam in clubs yesterday, and made a grand slam! Only that man Barabanoff spoilt the whole game for me again. We were playing—well, I said "No trumps" and he said "Pass." "Two in clubs," he passed again. I made it two in hearts. He said "Three in clubs," and just imagine, can you, what happened? I declared a little slam and he never showed his ace! If he had showed his ace, the villain, I should have declared a grand slam in no trumps!

LVOFF. Excuse me, I don't play cards, and so it is impossible for me to share your enthusiasm. When does the ceremony begin?

KOSICH. At once, I think. They are now bringing Zuzu to herself again. She is bellowing like a bull; she can't bear to see the money go.

LVOFF. And what about the daughter?

KOSICH. No, it is the money. She doesn't like this affair anyway. He is marrying her daughter, and that means he won't pay his debts for a long time. One can't sue one's son-in-law.

MARTHA, very much dressed up, struts across the stage past LVOFF and KOSICH. The latter bursts out laughing behind his hand. MARTHA looks around.

MARTHA. Idiot!

KOSICH digs her in the ribs and laughs loudly.

MARTHA. Boor!

KOSICH. [Laughing] The woman's head has been turned. Before she fixed her eye on a title she was like any other woman, but there is no coming near her now! [Angrily] A boor, indeed!

LVOFF. [Excitedly] Listen to me; tell me honestly, what do you think of Ivanoff?

KOSICH. He's no good at all. He plays cards like a lunatic. This is what happened last year during Lent: I, the Count, Borkin and he, sat down to a game of cards. I led a——

LVOFF [Interrupting him] Is he a good man?

KOSICH. He? Yes, he's a good one! He and the Count are a pair of trumps. They have keen noses for a good game. First, Ivanoff set his heart on the Jewess, then, when his schemes failed in that quarter, he turned his thoughts toward Zuzu's money-bags. I'll wager you he'll ruin Zuzu in a year. He will ruin Zuzu, and the Count will ruin Martha. They will gather up all the money they can lay hands on, and live happily ever after! But, doctor, why are you so pale to-day? You look like a ghost.

LVOFF. Oh, it's nothing. I drank a little too much yesterday.

Enter LEBEDIEFF with SASHA.

LEBEDIEFF. We can have our talk here. [To LVOFF and KOSICH] Go into the ball-room, you two old fogies, and talk to the girls. Sasha and I want to talk alone here.

KOSICH. [Snapping his fingers enthusiastically as he goes by SASHA] What a picture! A queen of trumps!

LEBEDIEFF. Go along, you old cave-dweller; go along.

KOSICH and LVOFF go out.

LEBEDIEFF. Sit down, Sasha, there—[He sits down and looks about him] Listen to me attentively and with proper respect. The fact is, your mother has asked me to say this, do you understand? I am not speaking for myself. Your mother told me to speak to you.

SASHA. Papa, do say it briefly!

LEBEDIEFF. When you are married we mean to give you fifteen thousand roubles. Please don't let us have any discussion about it afterward. Wait, now! Be quiet! That is only the beginning. The best is yet to come. We have allotted you fifteen thousand roubles, but in consideration of the fact that Nicholas owes your mother nine thousand, that sum will have to be deducted from the amount we mean to give you. Very well. Now, beside that——

SASHA. Why do you tell me all this?

LEBEDIEFF. Your mother told me to.

SASHA. Leave me in peace! If you had any respect for yourself or me you could not permit yourself to speak to me in this way. I don't want your money! I have not asked for it, and never shall.

LEBEDIEFF. What are you attacking me for? The two rats in Gogol's fable sniffed first and then ran away, but you attack without even sniffing.

SASHA. Leave me in peace, and do not offend my ears with your two-penny calculations.

LEBEDIEFF. [Losing his temper] Bah! You all, every one of you, do all you can to make me cut my throat or kill somebody. One of you screeches and fusses all day and counts every penny, and the other is so clever and humane and emancipated that she cannot understand her own father! I offend your ears, do I? Don't you realise that before I came here to offend your ears I was being torn to pieces over there, [He points to the door] literally drawn and quartered? So you cannot understand? You two have addled my brain till I am utterly at my wits' end; indeed I am! [He goes toward the door, and stops] I don't like this business at all; I don't like any thing about you—

SASHA. What is it, especially, that you don't like?

LEBEDIEFF. Everything, everything!

SASHA. What do you mean by everything?

LEBEDIEFF. Let me explain exactly what I mean. Everything displeases me. As for your marriage, I simply can't abide it. [He goes up to SASHA and speaks caressingly] Forgive me, little Sasha, this marriage may be a wise one; it may be honest and not misguided, nevertheless, there is something about the whole affair that is not right; no, not right! You are not marrying as other girls do; you are young and fresh and pure as a drop of water, and he is a widower, battered and worn. Heaven help him. I don't understand him at all. [He kisses his daughter] Forgive me for saying so, Sasha, but I am sure there is something crooked about this affair; it is making a great deal of talk. It seems people are saying that first Sarah died, and then suddenly Ivanoff wanted to marry you. [Quickly] But, no, I am like an old woman; I am gossiping like a magpie. You must not listen to me or any one, only to your own heart.

SASHA. Papa, I feel myself that there is something wrong about my marriage. Something wrong, yes, wrong! Oh, if you only knew how heavy my heart is; this is unbearable! I am frightened and ashamed to confess this; Papa darling, you must help me, for heaven's sake. Oh, can't you tell me what I should do?

LEBEDIEFF. What is the matter, Sasha, what is it?

SASHA. I am so frightened, more frightened than I have ever been before. [She glances around her] I cannot understand him now, and I never shall. He has not smiled or looked straight into my eyes once since we have been engaged. He is forever complaining and apologising for something; hinting at some crime he is guilty of, and trembling. I am so tired! There are even moments when I think—I think—that I do not love him as I should, and when he comes to see us, or talks to me, I get so tired! What does it mean, dear father? I am afraid.

LEBEDIEFF. My darling, my only child, do as your old father advises you; give him up!

SASHA. [Frightened] Oh! How can you say that?

LEBEDIEFF. Yes, do it, little Sasha! It will make a scandal, all the tongues in the country will be wagging about it, but it is better to live down a scandal than to ruin one's life.

SASHA. Don't say that, father. Oh, don't. I refuse to listen! I must crush such gloomy thoughts. He is good and unhappy and misunderstood. I shall love him and learn to understand him. I shall set him on his feet again. I shall do my duty. That is settled.

LEBEDIEFF. This is not your duty, but a delusion—

SASHA. We have said enough. I have confessed things to you that I have not dared to admit even to myself. Don't speak about this to any one. Let us forget it.

LEBEDIEFF. I am hopelessly puzzled, and either my mind is going from old age or else you have all grown very clever, but I'll be hanged if I understand this business at all.

Enter SHABELSKI.

SHABELSKI. Confound you all and myself, too! This is maddening!

LEBEDIEFF. What do you want?

SHABELSKI Seriously, I must really do something horrid and rascally, so that not only I but everybody else will be disgusted by it. I certainly shall find something to do, upon my word I shall! I have already told Borkin to announce that I am to be married. [He laughs] Everybody is a scoundrel and I must be one too!

LEBEDIEFF. I am tired of you, Matthew. Look here, man you talk in such a way that, excuse my saying so, you will soon find yourself in a lunatic asylum!

SHABELSKI. Could a lunatic asylum possibly be worse than this house, or any othe r? Kindly take me there at once. Please do! Everybody is wicked and futile and worthless and stupid; I am an object of disgust to myself, I don't believe a word I say——

LEBEDIEFF. Let me give you a piece of advice, old man; fill your mouth full of tow, light it, and blow at everybody. Or, better still, take your hat and go home. This is a wedding, we all want to enjoy ourselves and you are croaking like a raven. Yes, really.

SHABELSKI leans on the piano and begins to sob.

LEBEDIEFF. Good gracious, Matthew, Count! What is it, dear Matthew, old friend? Have I offended you? There, forgive me; I didn't mean to hurt you. Come, drink some water.

SHABELSKI. I don't want any water. [Raises his head.]

LEBEDIEFF. What are you crying about?

SHABELSKI. Nothing in particular; I was just crying.

LEBEDIEFF. Matthew, tell me the truth, what is it? What has happened?

SHABELSKI. I caught sight of that violoncello, and—and—I remembered the Jewess.

LEBEDIEFF. What an unfortunate moment you have chosen to remember her. Peace be with her! But don't think of her now.

SHABELSKI. We used to play duets together. She was a beautiful, a glorious woman.

SASHA sobs.

LEBEDIEFF. What, are you crying too? Stop, Sasha! Dear me, they are both howling now, and I—and I—Do go away; the guests will see you!

SHABELSKI. Paul, when the sun is shining, it is gay even in a cemetery. One can be cheerful even in old age if it is lighted by hope; but I have nothing to hope for—not a thing!

LEBEDIEFF. Yes, it is rather sad for you. You have no children, no money, no occupation. Well, but what is there to be done about it? [To SASHA] What is the matter with you, Sasha?

SHABELSKI. Paul, give me some money. I will repay you in the next world. I would go to Paris and see my wife's grave. I have given away a great deal of money in my life, half my fortune indeed, and I have a right to ask for some now. Besides, I am asking a friend.

LEBEDIEFF. [Embarrassed] My dear boy, I haven't a penny. All right though. That is to say, I can't promise anything, but you understand—very well, very well. [Aside] This is agony!

Enter MARTHA.

MARTHA. Where is my partner? Count, how dare you leave me alone? You are horrid! [She taps SHABELSKI on the arm with her fan]

SHABELSKI. [Impatiently] Leave me alone! I can't abide you!

MARTHA. [Frightened] How? What?

SHABELSKI. Go away!

MARTHA. [Sinks into an arm-chair] Oh! Oh! Oh! [She bursts into tears.]

Enter ZINAIDA crying.

ZINAIDA. Some one has just arrived; it must be one of the ushers. It is time for the ceremony to begin.

SASHA. [Imploringly] Mother!

LEBEDIEFF. Well, now you are all bawling. What a quartette! Come, come, don't let us have any more of this dampness! Matthew! Martha! If you go on like this, I—I—shall cry too. [Bursts into tears] Heavens!

ZINAIDA. If you don't need your mother any more, if you are determined not to obey her, I shall have to do as you want, and you have my blessing.

Enter IVANOFF, dressed in a long coat, with gloves on.

LEBEDIEFF This is the finishing touch! What do you want?

SHABELSKI. Why are you here?

IVANOFF. I beg your pardon, you must allow me to speak to Sasha alone.

LEBEDIEFF. The bridegroom must not come to see the bride before the wedding. It is time for you to go to the church.

IVANOFF. Paul, I implore you.

LEBEDIEFF shrugs his shoulders. LEBEDIEFF, ZINAIDA, SHABELSKI, and MARTHA go out.

SASHA. [Sternly] What do you want?

IVANOFF. I am choking with anger; I cannot speak calmly. Listen to me; as I was dressing just now for the wedding, I looked in the glass and saw how grey my temples were. Sasha, this must not be! Let us end this senseless comedy before it is too late. You are young and pure; you have all your life before you, but I——

SASHA. The same old story; I have heard it a thousand times and I am tired of it. Go quickly to the church and don't keep everybody waiting!

IVANOFF. I shall go straight home, and you must explain to your family somehow that there is to be no wedding. Explain it as you please. It is time we came to our senses. I have been playing the part of Hamlet and you have been playing the part of a noble and devoted girl. We have kept up the farce long enough.

SASHA. [Losing her temper] How can you speak to me like this? I won't have it.

IVANOFF. But I am speaking, and will continue to speak.

SASHA. What do you mean by coming to me like this? Your melancholy has become absolutely ridiculous!

IVANOFF. No, this is not melancholy. It is ridiculous, is it? Yes, I am laughing, and if it were possible for me to laugh at myself a thousand times more bitterly I should do so and set the whole world laughing, too, in derision. A fierce light has suddenly broken over my soul; as I looked into the glass just now, I laughed at myself, and nearly went mad with shame. [He laughs] Melancholy indeed! Noble grief! Uncontrollable sorrow! It only remains for me now to begin to write verses! Shall I mope and complain, sadden everybody I meet, confess that my manhood has gone forever, that I have decayed, outlived my purpose, that I have given myself up to cowardice and am bound hand and foot by this loathsome melancholy? Shall I confess all this when the sun is shining so brightly and when even the ants are carrying their little burdens in peaceful self-content? No, thanks. Can I endure the knowledge that one will look upon me as a fraud, while another pities me, a third lends me a helping hand, or worst of all, a fourth listens reverently to my sighs, looks upon me as a new Mahomet, and expects me to expound a new religion every moment? No, thank God for the pride and conscience he has left me still. On my way here I laughed at myself, and it seemed to me that the flowers and birds were laughing mockingly too.

SASHA. This is not anger, but madness!

IVANOFF. You think so, do you? No, I am not mad. I see things in their right light now, and my mind is as clear as your conscience. We love each other, but we shall never be married. It makes no difference how I rave and grow bitter by myself, but I have no right to drag another down with me. My melancholy robbed my wife of the last year of her life. Since you have been engaged to me you have forgotten how to laugh and have aged five years. Your father, to whom life was always simple and clear, thanks to me, is now unable to understand anybody. Wherever I go, whether hunting or visiting, it makes no difference, I carry depression, dulness, and discontent along with me. Wait! Don't interrupt me! I am bitter and harsh, I know, but I am stifled with rage. I cannot speak otherwise. I have never lied, and I never used to find fault with my lot, but since I have begun to complain of everything, I find fault with it involuntarily, and against my will. When I murmur at my fate every one who hears me is seized with the same disgust of life and begins to grumble too. And what a strange way I have of looking at things! Exactly as if I were doing the world a favour by living in it. Oh, I am contemptible.

SASHA. Wait a moment. From what you have just said, it is obvious that you are tired of your melancholy mood, and that the time has come for you to begin life afresh. How splendid!

IVANOFF. I don't see anything splendid about it. How can I lead a new life? I am lost forever. It is time we both understood that. A new life indeed!

SASHA. Nicholas, come to your senses. How can you say you are lost? What do you mean by such cynicism? No, I won't listen to you or talk with you. Go to the church!

IVANOFF. I am lost!

SASHA. Don't talk so loud; our guests will hear you!

IVANOFF. If an intelligent, educated, and healthy man begins to complain of his lot and go down-hill, there is nothing for him to do but to go on down until he reaches the bottom—there is no hope for him. Where could my salvation come from? How can I save myself? I cannot drink, because it makes my head ache. I never could write bad poetry. I cannot pray for strength and see anything lofty in the languor of my soul. Laziness is laziness and weakness weakness. I can find no other names for them. I am lost, I am lost; there is no doubt of that. [Looking around] Some one might come in; listen, Sasha, if you love me you must help me. Renounce me this minute; quickly!

SASHA. Oh, Nicholas! If you only knew how you are torturing me; what agony I have to endure for your sake! Good thoughtful friend, judge for yourself; can I possibly solve such a problem? Each day you put some horrible problem before me, each one more difficult than the last. I wanted to help you with my love, but this is martyrdom!

IVANOFF. And when you are my wife the problems will be harder than ever. Understand this: it is not love that is urging you to take this step, but the obstinacy of an honest nature. You have undertaken to reawaken the man in me and to save me in the face of every difficulty, and you are flattered by the hope of achieving your object. You are willing to give up now, but you are prevented from doing it by a feeling that is a false one. Understand yourself!

SASHA. What strange, wild reasoning! How can I give you up now? How can I? You have no mother, or sister, or friends. You are ruined; your estate has been destroyed; every one is speaking ill of you—

IVANOFF. It was foolish of me to come here; I should have done as I wanted to—

Enter LEBEDIEFF.

SASHA. [Running to her father] Father! He has rushed over here like a madman, and is torturing me! He insists that I should refuse to marry him; he says he doesn't want to drag me down with him. Tell him that I won't accept his generosity. I know what I am doing!

LEBEDIEFF. I can't understand a word of what you are saying. What generosity?

IVANOFF. This marriage is not going to take place.

SASHA. It is going to take place. Papa, tell him that it is going to take place.

LEBEDIEFF. Wait! Wait! What objection have you to the marriage?

IVANOFF. I have explained it all to her, but she refuses to understand me.

LEBEDIEFF. Don't explain it to her, but to me, and explain it so that I may understand. God forgive you, Nicholas, you have brought a great deal of darkness into our lives. I feel as if I were living in a museum; I look about me and don't understand anything I see. This is torture. What on earth can an old man like me do with you? Shall I challenge you to a duel?

IVANOFF. There is no need of a duel. All you need is a head on your shoulders and a knowledge of the Russian language.

SASHA. [Walks up and down in great excitement] This is dreadful, dreadful! Absolutely childish.

LEBEDIEFF. Listen to me, Nicholas; from your point of view what you are doing is quite right and proper, according to the rules of psychology, but I think this affair is a scandal and a great misfortune. I am an old man; hear me out for the last time. This is what I want to say to you: calm yourself; look at things simply, as every one else does; this is a simple world. The ceiling is white; your boots are black; sugar is sweet. You love Sasha and she loves you. If you love her, stay with her; if you don't, leave her. We shan't blame you. It is all perfectly simple. You are two healthy, intelligent, moral young people; thank God, you both have food and clothing—what more do you want? What if you have no money? That is no great misfortune—happiness is not bought with wealth. Of course your estate is mortgaged, Nicholas, as I know, and you have no money to pay the interest on the debt, but I am Sasha's father. I understand. Her mother can do as she likes—if she won't give any money, why, confound her, then she needn't, that's all! Sasha has just said that she does not want her part of it. As for your principles, Schopenhauer and all that, it is all folly. I have one hundred thousand roubles in the bank. [Looking around him] Not a soul in the house knows it; it was my grandmother's money. That shall be for you both. Take it, give Matthew two thousand—

[The guests begin to collect in the ball-room].

IVANOFF. It is no use discussing it any more, I must act as my conscience bids me.

SASHA. And I shall act as my conscience bids me—you may say what you please; I refuse to let you go! I am going to call my mother.

LEBEDIEFF. I am utterly puzzled.

IVANOFF. Listen to me, poor old friend. I shall not try to explain myself to you. I shall not tell you whether I am honest or a rascal, healthy or mad; you wouldn't understand me. I was young once; I have been eager and sincere and intelligent. I have loved and hated and believed as no one else has. I have worked and hoped and tilted against windmills with the strength of ten—not sparing my strength, not knowing what life was. I shouldered a load that broke my back. I drank, I worked, I excited myself, my energy knew no bounds. Tell me, could I have done otherwise? There are so few of us and so much to do, so much to do! And see how cruelly fate has revenged herself on me, who fought with her so bravely! I am a broken man. I am old at thirty. I have submitted myself to old age. With a heavy head and a sluggish mind, weary, used up, discouraged, without faith or love or an object in life, I wander like a shadow among other men, not knowing why I am alive or what it is that I want. Love seems to me to be folly, caresses false. I see no sense in working or playing, and all passionate speeches seem insipid and tiresome. So I carry my sadness with me wherever I go; a cold weariness, a discontent, a horror of life. Yes, I am lost for ever and ever. Before you stands a man who at thirty-five is disillusioned, wearied by fruitless efforts, burning with shame, and mocking at his own weakness. Oh, how my pride rebels against it all! What mad fury chokes me! [He staggers] I am staggering—my strength is failing me. Where is Matthew? Let him take me home.

[Voices from the ball-room] The best man has arrived!

Enter SHABELSKI.

SHABELSKI. In an old worn-out coat—without gloves! How many scornful glances I get for it! Such silly jokes and vulgar grins! Disgusting people.

Enter BORKIN quickly. He is carrying a bunch of flowers and is in a dress-coat. He wears a flower in his buttonhole.

BORKIN. This is dreadful! Where is he? [To IVANOFF] They have been waiting for you for a long time in the church, and here you are talking philosophy! What a funny chap you are. Don't you know you must not go to church with the bride, but alone, with me? I shall then come back for her. Is it possible you have not understood that? You certainly are an extraordinary man!

Enter LVOFF.

LVOFF. [To IVANOFF] Ah! So you are here? [Loudly] Nicholas Ivanoff, I denounce you to the world as a scoundrel!

IVANOFF. [Coldly] Many thanks!

BORKIN. [To LVOFF] Sir, this is dastardly! I challenge you to a duel!

LVOFF. Monsieur Borkin, I count it a disgrace not only to fight with you, but even to talk to you! Monsieur Ivanoff, however, can receive satisfaction from me whenever he chooses!

SHABELSKI. Sir, I shall fight you!

SASHA. [To LVOFF] Why, oh why, have you insulted him? Gentlemen, I beg you, let him tell me why he has insulted him.

LVOFF. Miss Sasha, I have not insulted him without cause. I came here as a man of honour, to open your eyes, and I beg you to listen to what I have to tell you.

SASHA. What can you possibly have to tell me? That you are a man of honour? The whole world knows it. You had better tell me on your honour whether you understand what you have done or not. You have come in here as a man of honour and have insulted him so terribly that you have nearly killed me. When you used to follow him like a shadow and almost keep him from living, you were convinced that you were doing your duty and that you were acting like a man of honour. When you interfered in his private affairs, maligned him and criticised him; when you sent me and whomever else you could, anonymous letters, you imagined yourself to be an honourable man! And, thinking that that too was honourable, you, a doctor, did not even spare his dying wife or give her a moment's peace from your suspicions. And no matter what violence, what cruel wrong you committed, you still imagined yourself to be an unusually honourable and clear-sighted man.

IVANOFF. [Laughing] This is not a wedding, but a parliament! Bravo! Bravo!

SASHA. [To LVOFF] Now, think it over! Do you see what sort of a man you are, or not? Oh, the stupid, heartless people! [Takes IVANOFF by the hand] Come away from here Nicholas! Come, father, let us go!

IVANOFF. Where shall we go? Wait a moment. I shall soon put an end to the whole thing. My youth is awake in me again; the former Ivanoff is here once more.

[He takes out a revolver.]

SASHA. [Shrieking] I know what he wants to do! Nicholas, for God's sake!

IVANOFF. I have been slipping down-hill long enough. Now, halt! It is time to know what honour is. Out of the way! Thank you, Sasha!

SASHA. [Shrieking] Nicholas! For God's sake hold him!

IVANOFF. Let go! [He rushes aside, and shoots himself.]

The curtain falls.

www.ingramcontent.com/pod-product-compliance
Lightning Source LLC
La Vergne TN
LVHW090039080526
838202LV00046B/3887